A RENEGADE'S JOURNEY TO STILLNESS

A Renegade's Journey to Stillness

A memoir of family, healing and growth

MARITA ESPADA

Swordstone

Publishing

Paperback: 979-8-9988578-0-5
Ebook: 979-8-9988578-1-2

Library of Congress Control Number: 2025912336

To my beloved wife, Irene, who has always been my greatest supporter. Though I began my journey toward stillness alone, it is with you that I have discovered life's most beautiful adventures.

To my sweet pup, Riley, whose playful spirit and loving heart always lift me up.

And to anyone feeling hopeless, lost or alone, this book is for you. Never give up.

CONTENTS

NOTE TO READERS

The story you are about to read is true. It's my recollection of my life; others in the story might remember things differently. Names have been changed to protect the privacy of those in my life. As much as I enjoy helping others, this is my story and should not be taken as medical advice or a substitute for working with a professional. This book is not an alternative to health care, medical, or nutritional therapy services, and the information herein should not be used to diagnose, treat, prevent or cure any mental or emotional issue, disease, or condition. This book contains sensitive themes, including references to suicide and murder. These topics may be distressing for some readers, so please proceed with caution. If you or someone you know is struggling with these issues, support is available, resources within the United States are listed below:

- **National Suicide Prevention Lifeline:** Call 988 or text "HELLO" to 741741 for free, confidential support 24/7.
- **Crisis Text Line:** Text HOME to 741741 for free, confidential crisis counseling.
- **The Trevor Project (LGBTQ+ support):** Call 1-866-488-7386 or text START to 678678.

Please reach out to these services for help if needed.

With that said, my intention for this book extends beyond providing an engaging reading experience; I also aimed to create practical resources for those who feel compelled to apply its insights. To that end, I've included curated tools at the end of select chapters—resources that have proven valuable in my own journey.

You can find them all on my website:
https://maritaespada.com
or scan the QR code below:

PREFACE

Develop enough courage so that you can stand up for yourself and then stand up for somebody else.
—MAYA ANGELOU

B y the time I turned six, I had already been labeled and diagnosed with learning disabilities that marked me as different before I even knew what that meant. By fourteen, I had been through several surgeries, enough to become familiar with pain. It showed me how to manage it, live with it, and keep moving on. At eighteen, I experienced the raw truth of loneliness when my friends and family learned that I was gay. By nineteen, death stared me in the face and I stared right back at it. From the very beginning, life handed me a script I did not ask for. As the poster child of a minority, I checked all the boxes you can think of and then some.

What you're about to read isn't your typical memoir. Though practical tools and strategies are woven throughout, at its core, it's still a memoir, a story of my life. As I worked through writing this story, the more passionate I became about storytelling and the true power behind it. If we all share our stories, if we are more vulnerable, our collective empathy will grow organically, allowing us to walk in each other's shoes. For a second, we would all come to the realization that we are not that different from one another. Storytelling helps us learn, grow wiser, and deepen our empathy. Through the characters we meet whether imagined or real we connect with their journeys. By reading their words we step into their stories gaining insight into lives beyond our own.

Accordingly, I didn't set out to write this book to feed my ego or because I've found all the answers. Rather, I have learned not to speak in absolutes, as life itself is not absolute. I wrote it hoping that my story will help others. In writing my memoir, I've learned this process is not for the faint of heart. It can heal, but it's also a stark reminder of your role as the central character in those stories from your past, that challenges you to consider what you've learned from those experiences.

At its core, this is the book I wish I had in 2012. Like many people, I was living on autopilot trapped in the same stories I kept telling myself unaware of how deeply they shaped my reality. For some, it feels impossible to break free. For others, there is not even the awareness that they are disconnected from themselves from life and from the world around them. That was me too until I came to understand that the most important relationship we will ever have is the one we have with ourselves. So why not be fully awake for it?

As you'll soon see, I learned that the hard way.

It all began in 2012. I had no idea what to do with my life, no direction and I couldn't shake the constant feeling of self-loathing, hopelessness, loneliness, and being lost. I didn't know it then, but I was at the edge of a cliff, looking down while the floor beneath me began to crumble. After several near-death experiences, a plan began to unravel in my mind, and I journaled throughout all those years, creating the story that you are about to read. A story about family bonds, loss, grief, healing, growth and learning to start all over again. The trajectory of my life is not a miracle by any stretch, but I'm grateful for the opportunities that either presented themselves to me and the ones I had the courage to create. I'm thankful for what I have been able to achieve so far. Even more so, when 32.2% of children with any combined type learning disabilities dropout of highschool, compared to 15% of those without learning disabilities. Those that decide to attend college and are accepted, only 28% graduate. As compelling research shows, children with learning disabilities end up in adulthood with lower levels of education, poor social functioning and less success than their colleagues once they enter the workforce. This can at times be complicated even further, when the nuclear family unit separates at a very young age, it disrupts the child's routine and safety. As I internalized all of this, the years ahead created an unspoken blueprint to unravel the internal pain that somehow had developed.

I can still recall my earliest memory, which would be the correlation between the data points above and my own storyline. When I was four years old, I walked through what was once my parents' bedroom, to find the light green accordion closet doors wide open. As I peeked inside the closet, I found it completely empty. I was too young to fully understand that feeling, but I remember loneliness slowly creeping in and feeling as empty as that closet.

INTRODUCTION

In order to understand life, first you must live it.

—ERNEST HEMINGWAY

If you told me in my early twenties that I would write and publish a book, I would have spit laughed my beer and moved on to the next party. Back then I was the polar opposite of a writer or planner or a responsible human being for that matter. I lived life as if every day was going to be my last. I often would throw caution to the wind at least until it inevitably came back like a boomerang to slap me in the face, which happened often. I still have some of the scars to prove it. A friend from university once told me, "I don't remember the last time you stayed home on a weekend. You always have somewhere to be or something to do."

That wasn't an exaggeration, I would pack my Fridays and Saturdays with adrenaline-filled adventures, clubbing, and house parties. To wrap it up, I would nurse my hangovers at the beach on Sundays. Part of this was because I didn't want to be alone with my thoughts. I didn't want to see the reality of certain aspects of my life, including some of my personality traits. In some ways, I was always running away from myself. But that, too, eventually caught up with me. I had run so far away from myself that I didn't even know who I was anymore.

My story begins on a small, yet vibrant island, where the people are sun-kissed year-round, filled with natural beauty and its immersive culture that can bring anyone in, as the sound of Latin music fills the space around you -- Puerto Rico, where I was born and raised. Growing up on the island taught me many lessons, some I didn't appreciate until I was much older.

I grew up knowing that one day I would need to leave the island. I always carried an intense feeling that there was more waiting for me beyond the small world my island offered. But when the time finally came to go, I realized I hadn't fully appreciated the place I had called home for twenty-five years. I didn't expect that leaving would mean risking a disconnect from my culture, that I would crave the flavors of my favorite dishes, or that I would miss walking the cobblestone streets of Old San Juan with family, friends, and a piragua in hand. A piragua is a popular frozen dessert from Puerto Rico made of shaved ice topped with fruit-flavored syrups. Unlike the round American snow cone, piraguas are pyramid shaped and uniquely Puerto Rican. I didn't realize those simple moments would never fully return once I moved.

Guilt and sadness filled my body as my mother and aunt drove me to the airport in 2013 to move to San Francisco.

What's a Renegade?

You didn't ask but here we are anyway. It's finally time to talk about that one word that let's be honest kind of steals the spotlight in the title. If you look up the word renegade you'll find a range of definitions a rebel a defector someone who abandons a cause. But being a renegade doesn't have to carry a negative connotation. At its best a renegade is someone bold and visionary someone who challenges convention and disrupts the status quo in pursuit of something better. It's about moral courage the willingness to act on your values even when it's uncomfortable unpopular or risky. A renegade is someone who pushes back against constructs that can be used to express ideas. While most people might follow social constructs and values that are pushed on them or inherited from society and family renegades look to shine a light otherwise.

In truth, we all have renegade moments. We all encounter chapters in life where we choose to step off the expected path, to speak up, to break free. Maybe you're in one of those moments right now. In what ways are you quietly or boldly pushing back? What social norms, expectations, or beliefs are you questioning? Those instincts to resist, to speak out, to stand tall they're signs your inner renegade is alive and well. The question is are you listening?

Think about the moments that shaped you the most. Chances are, those were your renegade beliefs speaking to you. Times when you were following a vision no one else could see but you. These experiences don't just mark turning points they define who we are and the direction we choose to walk. This memoir is my attempt to trace those moments in my own life to explore the renegade beliefs that moved me to act, to speak, to change. I also invite you to reflect on your own journey as you read. Throughout the book, we will explore how to define these values for yourself, live them with moral courage, use them to foster genuine conversations with others, and build a life that truly reflects who you are.

Because when we understand the values that move us to act with courage especially in the face of difficulty we get closer to understanding ourselves. And in a time when studies show moral courage is in decline it's never been more important. It's what sparks genuine conversations, fuels social change, and connects us on a human level.

Without renegade beliefs, we wouldn't have revolutionary breakthroughs in science, justice, or the arts. Some people know what their renegade beliefs are and live by them with unwavering clarity. Others spend a lifetime trying to name them.

Where are you?

Where to Start?

My mother, Tibby, immigrated to Puerto Rico from Cuba as part of Operation Pedro Pan, a secret mass exodus that brought over 14,000 unaccompanied Cuban children to the United States between 1960 and 1962. Parents sent their children away out of fear that Fidel Castro and the Communist Party planned to strip them of their parental rights and place minors in communist indoctrination centers. The operation was named Pedro Pan, Spanish for Peter Pan, a reference to the fictional boy who was taken from home and never grew up, symbolizing the painful separation from family and the lost innocence of a childhood cut short. Operation Pedro Pan remains the largest recorded migration of unaccompanied minors in the Western Hemisphere. My mother and aunt were separated from their parents for a year while living in Florida with my grandmother's friend, who unknowingly to them did not treat them as kindly as they had hoped. They barely spoke English but were thrown into this American life. After reuniting with my grandparents, they relocated to build a new life in Puerto Rico. Once they settled in Puerto Rico, my mother, my aunt, and my grandparents lived in a small apartment with a hundred-dollar loan that my grandfather received from a friend to begin rebuilding their life. After many rentals, eventually through my grandfather's yearning to prosper and provide for his family, he bought a home, one that we still own today. My mother and my aunt were thirteen at the time and after many years, welcomed Puerto Rico as their home. They went to school, made friends, and since Puerto Rican culture is similar to Cuban culture, with time they blended in well. After graduating from high school, my mother attended the University of Puerto Rico, where she met my father, Mario, in a social club for twins. I'm serious, who would have thought universities had so many enrolled twins that they could form an entire social club around it?

Shortly after graduating university in the mid 1970s, they tied the knot and started figuring out adult life together, navigating work, family expectations, and settling into a new routine.

Circa 1974

I was born in 1986, just as Governor Rafael Hernández Colón began his second term, and the island was in an economic boom. During that same year, my parents also purchased their first home in a town called Guaynabo. When we first moved in, the surrounding area was nothing but mountains and fresh air, the countryside. A small, quaint town, Guaynabo was a place where everyone knew each other. It seemed like the perfect place to raise a family.

Circa 1986

If you visit Guaynabo now, it's a popular city with many malls, serving a major business district.

I grew up in a deeply Catholic middle-class family, we lived life according to the Bible for most, if not all, my life. I didn't realize it at the time, but religion was the basis of how we lived. It wasn't uncommon for my family to just "pray away" an issue or problem that came our way.

I don't remember a time without Mass on Sunday or everything we said and did revolving around the phrase, "What would Jesus do?" In my early twenties, I stumbled upon Buddhism and started talking openly about it, sharing what I was learning on my spiritual journey. Based on their reactions, you'd think I'd just robbed a liquor store and stabbed someone all in one go. Which, just for the record, I didn't... or did I? Guess you'll have to keep reading and find out, aren't you curious now? To them, I either followed the religion that my family believed in, or I didn't believe in any religion at all.

I hadn't thought much about coming of age in Puerto Rico until I started to write this book. Growing up on the island in the 1990s and early 2000s always felt like a great adventure. I had the privilege to live in an eternal state of summer with a nightlife that can only be understood if you have experienced it yourself. Puerto Rico's music and its people are two of the best things the island has to offer. Its history and culture are so rich, full of color, life, and laughter.

However, despite its breathtaking beauty, the island had its share of issues. It wasn't uncommon to lose electricity every week, which my family still encounters today. I still remember cheering when the power returned hoping for the first ten to fifteen minutes, we wouldn't lose it again. We'd often lose power for up to three weeks, a month, or even longer after a hurricane. We somehow learned how to live with it. We would make our morning coffee on a moka pot on a small gas stove and cook dinners on a charcoal grill outside, spending our time in the sun and playing dominoes until dark while the coquis sang in the background.

Coquis are a small native frog known for singing loudly around the island at night. They are so named because of the noise they make. The *co* sound helps male frogs repel other males that might try to establish themselves in their territory, while the *kee* sound attracts females. After years of hearing them, I struggled to get used to the cars, police sirens, and the overall city noise of San Francisco. I truly missed drifting into sleep to the sound of the coquis in the background, the comforting sound of home.

Looking back at those times on the island, I feel so grateful for them. A hurricane could pause life, and people would get to talk to one another and truly be together. It was a time when neighbors came together as a community to share resources. No one was focused on the latest trends, expensive clothes, or cars. We just laughed, played board games, and enjoyed the simple pleasures.

At night, when it was hot, I would shower in freezing-cold water. If we didn't have water at the time, I would bathe with cold water that we kept in a bucket in the bathtub. Then I would lay on the tile floor with a pillow and a blanket because it was the only way to stay cool throughout the night. I don't remember ever complaining, but I'm sure I did. Those experiences have stayed with me throughout my life, and I truly believe that I have learned to adjust to changes quicker than most others as a result.

Puerto Rico is a commonwealth of the United States, but it doesn't always feel as if it's part of the United States of America. I often compared Puerto Rican life to the life of the typical American I saw on TV and felt constricted by the lack of opportunities that I saw in Puerto Rico. This is our lifelong dilemma, isn't it? Does your environment limit the opportunities that are available to you or what if you're still able to create opportunities regardless of your environment?

It took me years of reflection and writing this book to truly understand what that meant for me.

My grandparents had a picture of my older brother and me sitting on a bench at Disney World in Florida during the winter of 1990. We had neon jackets, my older brother with big glasses, two kids full of innocence and absolutely no idea that I would resent the picture as an adult. I always thought of it as a memento of my first trip to Disney World as a child, but I later learned there was another meaning to the picture. It wasn't simply a fun trip; it had been a distraction from my parents' crumbling marriage. Learning what was really going on ruined the picture for me as an adult. It's as if we froze a pivotal moment in my family's life, a day we probably didn't need a picture to remember.

The Impact of Absence

My father was in and out of my life and barely to be found in my childhood photo album. Papi, the storyteller, the musician, the part-time magician, the serial hobbyist, the womanizer, the foodie. As a child, on those rare Saturdays that he'd pick me up, we would drive around the island by the beach. We would stop in *chinchorros* (places with music and food where locals spend their time) as we ate *bacalaitos, alcapurrias, cuajitos* and *pinchos*. He passed all of that to me and then some. At five foot seven, he is not a tall man, but what lacks in height, he makes up for in personality. In the 1980s and '90s, he sported a thick black mustache and even today he never wears sneakers, only dress shoes, dress pants, and a neatly tucked in button down shirt. If there's a mirror nearby, he meticulously brushes his hair back with a folded hairbrush that he often carries in his pocket.

Circa 10's

He is obsessed with watches, never leaving the house without one and keeping an immense collection throughout the years. His music of choice is a mix of old-school Puerto Rican salsa of El Gran Combo, Gilberto Santarosa, Tito Nieves, and Héctor Lavoe. Later in life, he found a passion and admiration for Andrea Bocelli, and that's all you hear throughout the house.

Papi, always running away from the life he had created as soon as the routine got boring, or things got hard. He is always chasing the next best thing, the next thrillride that life has to offer. With that lifestyle comes a larger-than-life personality. When he enters a room, he wants to be noticed, and people always do. His goal is always to find ways to be the center of attention in any social event. I didn't realize it when I was younger, but he is a textbook narcissist. Either you agree with him, or you are wrong. Either you are this one type of person, the high socioeconomic individual, with a well known powerful career path such as lawyer, doctor, politician or he will look down on you. His sense of grandiosity and lack of empathy created many issues for me. Even though he was not very present in my life, I often heard that we had the same mannerisms, personality, and temperament. That has always been hard for me to digest.

When I get passionate about something like a story or a point of view, I often raise my voice and become very animated with my hands. I try to recreate the story for my listeners and have them relive it with me. This tends to be well received by strangers or those I've met as an adult, but with my family, it's usually considered loud or obnoxious. Over time I began to question myself and my personality, wondering whether I made people feel the way my father made me feel.

He tends to be very selfish and does things that only benefit him. This is something that I didn't grasp until well into my thirties. I grew up feeling angry toward him and my circumstances, but in retrospect, I wish I had found ways to work through that earlier.

As I became a young adult, my father and I were able to find some peace within our relationship. In the end, I gave myself permission to set boundaries around the type of relationship I feel comfortable having with him. As of now, we don't have much of one, and I sometimes question whether it's the correct decision. As you get older, you start to find your place in the world and put in the work to finally feel at ease and genuinely happy in your own skin.

Speaking with him always stole that confidence away from me. I would walk away feeling destroyed, worthless, and ultimately that was a price I wasn't willing to pay.

I remember meeting my friends' parents or hearing them talk about their relationships, and feeling a quick wave of jealousy, wishing I had something like that. It does provide some relief to know that I could forgive what happened when I was younger, but I do not forget it. If I forgot my past, those moments would never solidify themselves as life lessons.

Twin Mothers

This dynamic with my father fed into my parents' relationship struggles. They were never on the same page, or even the same chapter. My mother wanted to create a family and dreamed of the day my father would become a family man. My father was solemnly focused on his career and living life as an eternal bachelor, despite being married with two children at home. His medical and military careers, hobbies, and entrepreneurial ventures consumed his time. They were always playing tug-of-war with their aspirations, and we lived like this until 1990, when my mom had had enough and asked for a divorce. Enter the trip to Disney— "The Happiest Place on Earth." Because nothing says "fresh start" like a giant mouse handing you an ice cream shaped like himself! Shout out to Mickey-shaped ice cream on a hot summer day after a divorce.

Circa 1990

My mother and aunt have always been constants in my life, by DNA I technically have two mothers. Although they're my twin mothers, they're very different in their ways. My mother, stuck in a constant balancing act, was always cooking meals and making sure everyone had everything they needed, trying to be an involved mother as she navigated what her new single life meant for her. Mami, the rule follower, organizer, maker of arts and crafts, the penny pincher, the queen of hugs. With her short brown hair and tendency to always wear makeup, even when she had a mop in hand cleaning, she made sure the house was always spotless. When she wasn't cleaning, she was doing laundry. I don't think she particularly liked to cook, but she would often whip us up quick meals, usually consisting of chicken with rice and beans or picadillo with olives. Once she was done cleaning, she would sit back and relax on the couch to watch Lifetime. At night, she would spend her time reading in bed, often falling asleep with a book in hand. She was always trying to make a dollar stretch and would often purchase her clothes on clearance so I could buy a nice T-shirt for Casual Friday at school. At five feet tall, she was shorter than me by the time I entered seventh grade. I would pick her up with a tight bear hug until she would laugh and yell out, "No, Marita, Marita put me down!"

My aunt is more of an active listener. She'll lend you an ear and provide advice; I think she is more of a researcher at heart. Ask her a question and twenty-four hours later, you have a full book report on that subject. She is always willing to lend a helping hand to those in need. She would often come over to our house for dinner and sit at the kitchen table to gossip with Mami as she made dinner. After we all ate, they would make their way to the living room to watch a telenovela together. They always have the same haircut, dress alike, and to this day are inseparable.

My aunt, or Titi as I call her, is always adorned in jewelry, necklaces, rings, and colored string bracelets that I gave her as a child. She used to tell stories with a beer in her hand, and somewhere along the way, she graduated to doing the same with a glass of wine.

Before I was born, my mother wanted a girl. Someone to go shopping with, someone to talk with about boys. She longed for that mother-daughter bond. Then in 1985, after craving soda and brownies for a long time, she found out she was pregnant and due the summer of 1986.

What she didn't expect was who I would turn out to be—a girl who wanted to ride bikes with the boys, play sports, and win. I was extremely competitive and obsessed with being number one. She had a daughter who didn't get good grades and could not sit still in class. I took more pride in learning how to build things than in learning how to apply lipstick or which shoes to wear.

My mother got a child who, in fifth grade, used liquid white-out to mark herself a designated pickup spot because obviously the sidewalk was prime real estate and I wasn't about to share it with the commoners. While other kids waited patiently, I had my own exclusive curbside suite. Velvet ropes were the only thing missing. From a very early age, I was the textbook definition of an alpha, leading the charge, calling the shots, and probably annoying everyone around me with my "I've got this" attitude.

My mother, whether she liked it or not, got a daughter who not only looked like, but also acted like, the man she had divorced. It was not until much later in my life that I came to realize this is most likely the reason we struggled to have a deep and real relationship. I reminded her and my brother, Mario Jr. too much of the man that had hurt them. It always felt like an uphill battle to connect with them.

Parental Figures

My grandfather Fernando was the father figure that I did not have. A Cuban immigrant who moved his family to Puerto Rico after Fidel Castro assumed military and political power He was a hard-working man who became a respected professional with only a fourth-grade education.

His family could only afford to send his older brother, Carlos, to school. When his brother was done with his books, my grandfather would read them and absorb as much as he could. He started his career in the mailroom of the International Telephone and Telegraph Corporation (ITT), climbing the corporate ladder with nothing but pure grit and dedication. On April 15, 1981, he became the vice president of ITT's Caribbean and Virgin Islands group. Once he was able to purchase his own home in Puerto Rico, he had a home office where he would spend most of his day. Even after being retired for years, he still loved to work from his desk.

My *abuelo* was always listening to the news on the radio, writing, and doing crossword puzzles. Though a man of few words, he was very smart. My grandmother Maya would often say, "He just pushes paper back and forth to keep himself busy." But the truth is that he was always learning something new, whether it was French as a third language or completing family trees for the younger generations. He was very proud of his heritage and family background. I think he wanted to do everything he could to keep history alive for us. At the same time, my *abuela* was the definition of class. She would always wear high heels, dresses, and full makeup, even when going to the local grocery store. She made the best Cuban rice pudding and *frituritas*, hands down. Whenever she was about to make them, she would take out the same white ceramic bowl and fold a single paper towel in half to help soak up the grease from frying them. I would sit at the kitchen table in the same wood and wicker chair as always and watch impatiently until she was done. Her house was always impeccably clean, and she strived to teach me manners growing up. She taught me how to set a table, how to introduce myself to strangers, and how to treat others with empathy. She tried, bless her heart, to teach me not to ask for candy when we visited her friend's house. Spoiler alert: It didn't work. I was basically a walking sugar request. She was slow to anger and warmed any room she entered with her smile and charm. As part of her morning routine, she would apply moisturizer and lightly tap and stretch her face to prevent wrinkles. As a kid, I would stand next to her and pretend to do the same in a childish manner, not really understanding what she was doing.

Sadly, my abuela passed away when I was a senior in high school after many years of battling Alzheimer's. She struggled to remember us, and when she passed away, my grandfather struggled to learn how to live life without her. She was undeniably the glue of the family. Their relationship was the definition of true love, at least to me as a young child. They built a life together in Cuba when they were young, and years later they had to rebuild their entire life again in Puerto Rico. They had to send my mother and aunt to Florida when first escaping communism in Cuba and couldn't reunite for a full year. I remember my grandfather watching Fidel Castro on television in his living room, sitting in his big, soft, brown-fabric recliner—the same one I caught my finger on when I was four as I was playing with the mechanical reclining parts. I still have the scar from the four stitches they had to put in my dangling finger. My grandfather would sit calmly in his recliner as he listened to how his island was being destroyed by Castro, but he always managed to keep his composure, even when it was hard for him.

His home office featured an entire wall of books, with classical music always playing softly in the background. Every so often, he would sneak in a bit of Cuban salsa, adding a lively touch to the atmosphere. He was a classy, smart, and compassionate person. If you asked people who knew him, they would say he was a very serious and grumpy man, but I rarely saw that side of him. I believe he had a soft spot for me, as grandfathers do for their grandchildren. He was always looking to further educate himself. It's because of him that I continue to find ways to be more mindful and explore how to live a more meaningful and fulfilling life.

My sense of being an eternal student of life comes from him and his passion for learning and making things better. He had so many systems dictating how things should work, and if he needed a tool that he could not buy, he would build it himself. When I was about eight years old, he made a machine to crush soda cans. When he had enough cans, we would take them in a big black trash bag to get recycled. If I collected most of them, he would let me keep the five cents per can. He wasn't doing it for the money. We lived a comfortable life at this point. He was just ahead of his time and wanted to recycle to protect the world for the next generation.

He taught me how to play dominoes and Chinese checkers, and even how to read Morse code. If the day was nice enough, he would often play catch with me. I don't remember him ever saying a word about me not wanting to play with dolls or other toys that were made exclusively for my gender assigned at birth. He never made me feel like I was different, even though he was a very religious man. He would occasionally take me to McDonald's to order a Happy Meal as a treat. This was back in the 1990s when you had to choose between the girls' Happy Meal and the boys' Happy Meal for the "right" toy, and I always wanted the boys'. When the cashier would ask again, "You said boys' Happy Meal? You have a girl," my grandfather would calmly respond, "I know, we will have the boys' Happy Meal, thank you."

Gay was never a label I wanted to wear. Not because I'm not proud of who I am, but because I have been labeled as one thing or another my entire life. Through my journey to stillness, I created my own tools and systems, just as my grandfather did. These systems have helped me recognize those labels for what they are and to see them in another light rather than let my anger and frustrations take over. I'm not going to lie, I do still feel frustrated at times, mostly because the only label that I ever wanted to wear was *human being*. But as a society, we have created labels and made people fit into these boxes, whether it's for power, selfishness, or just history repeating itself. The harmful effects of labels permeate generations, creating trauma and holding weight on our self-identities. The moment a child is conceived, a label is provided to them for their gender, and even before they are born, people are planning their lives based on such gender, like interests, clothes, toys, and future plans. Furthermore, these social labels come with set expectations over things that we cannot control such as gender, sexual orientation, race, and more specifically for children, their social class, as this tends to be an ascribed status that is beyond an individual's control. These labels hold within them beliefs that we might not necessarily want to follow. On our own, we need to bring a level of awareness when those labels are placed upon us. We need to break them down. Find a place for our own renegade beliefs. We can work on this at an individual level, but one person alone cannot reshape our society. We all need to come together. Take a moment to consider your personal history. What tools and systems do you currently have in your personal life? Life is unexpected and at times those systems, tools, philosophies, and strategies can help us move through, from moment to moment.

1

A RENEGADE ORIGIN STORY

It is not the length of life, but the depth.
—RALPH WALDO EMERSON

From the outside looking in, things seemed as they should have been in my early twenties, and happiness was sure to follow. This is what we often assume of other people we run into who look happy. You might see them sipping a latte and laughing with their friends at the local coffee shop or taking a stroll as they approach a restaurant for dinner.

This is probably what others thought of me. As most twenty-two-year-olds didn't have half of what I had: a two bedroom apartment, a dog, a decent savings account, a used but dependable car, two part-time jobs. I was also a full-time student getting my bachelor's in business and information systems at the Metropolitan University of Puerto Rico.

I had gone back and forth many times on what to study and even started several other career paths. I switched universities twice and my majors three times. My apartment was small and old, and to park my car, I had to drive through a dirt lot. It was walking distance from a McDonald's, and with the amount of money I was making at the time, I became a regular customer. Like many struggling university students, it was extremely convenient for me to grab food there, and I made it my designated recovery center after a night of partying.

My dating life, meanwhile, was going well, or as well as it could go, I suppose. That said, later I would find myself standing in that same half-empty apartment after my girlfriend left me, leaving nothing, but a note on the kitchen table. My days consisted of waking up at 4:00 a.m. to deliver two hundred newspapers before my actual day really started. I would go to the pickup location and use rubber bands to wrap the papers up one by one to throw them from my car window to people's houses. I must say, I got pretty good at it. I had some Michelle Obama arms before the term existed. Four days out of seven, I would also work in retail, not getting home until 11:00 p.m. The next morning, I would rise and do it all over again. Throughout my twenties, I worked at many restaurants as a waiter, in retail at Party City, Office Max, a record store and in a full-time role in a title loan business. From all these jobs I either got fired for being unable to work on call shifts or I left voluntarily, because I would find a new role that would pay a little more.

I barely had time to do my homework, but somehow, I got really good at squeezing it into the tiniest pockets of time. I often felt overworked and stressed, but I kept pushing through, convincing myself that tomorrow would be better. Still, there were times when I wondered if I'd ever not feel exhausted, or if I'd ever feel truly whole. I convinced myself that if I worked hard enough, everything would fall into place, happiness, success, all of it. I would go to bed exhausted, thinking happiness was just around the corner. I was doing everything I should, so why wasn't it here? Was it waiting for an engraved invitation from me? Why wouldn't happiness want to join the party? After all, I would throw some of the best parties, so much so that they wouldn't end until after the police were called.

We live our lives with a checklist, one we inherited from our family, friends, and society. Some people decide to throw the checklist to the wind and carve their own path. But I never considered that as an option. I was never exposed to people who did that, and even if I was, my family would've said anything to convince me it was the wrong path. In Puerto Rico, you had to work hard at all times. You had to always be prepared; otherwise, you would struggle to make ends meet. The doors of opportunity were slim, and most of the time I needed to create my own door first before trying to walk through it.

On the other hand, those who decide to follow the checklist often assume that once every item is accounted for, happiness, fulfillment, and success will follow. It's only later in life that other paths reveal themselves, like invisible ink slowly becoming visible on a blank page. Until then, we spend so much of our lives chasing after success and material items that we lose ourselves along the way. We, in a way, give permission to others around us to tell us what success looks like and what we need to do to achieve it.

We know when the next iPhone will be released, we know how to keep up with the Kardashians, and even what award show is coming up next, but we don't know our values or what we stand for. That is what happened to me throughout my twenties. I didn't understand why I felt so lost, but at the same time, I didn't know what my values were. I lost myself in all the noise, but eventually, I was determined to find my way back. It all started with defining my values, which I began to uncover with time.

Our personal values tend to change as we grow. What's important to you as a teenager will be different from what you value most in adulthood. These values change based on your experiences. Each individual's values are unique to them. This means it's all about making a commitment to ourselves to review and redefine them as we grow and evolve.

A Renegade Is Born

I grew up with multiple learning disabilities and often felt like I was falling behind. I carried a quiet shame, not just for struggling in school while others seemed to thrive. There was also a deeper discomfort with who I was, something I wouldn't begin to understand until much later. This was the beginning of years of self-loathing, destructive behaviors, and depression. I spent many years, if not most of my childhood, in after-school programs that would help me with homework and managing my learning disabilities. During one of those tutoring sessions, they placed me in a tiny cubicle and played a tape of multiplication tables on repeat, as if sheer repetition could somehow "fix" my learning disabilities. It felt more like punishment than support. No matter how many times I heard the numbers, I still couldn't memorize them and worse, I started to believe there was something deeply wrong with me. The tutors weren't certified teachers, nor were they trained to work with kids like me. After months of enduring this, my mother finally listened when I told her what was happening. This was the first step of how the renegade was born. I pushed back on the shame that others wanted me to own, on the labels they wanted me to wear. I pushed back on the belittling, and to this day, I'm still the first one to stand up against any kind of bullying or abuse.

This was a point in my life that shaped my future. This was a core renegade chapter for me even though I was still too young to recognize it at the time.

From kindergarten to twelfth grade, I moved to a total of four schools. At the first school I attended, my mother was politely told that they could not help me any longer and that I should leave the school. I had been diagnosed with ADHD in first grade, and I was not at the same level as my peers, a real drawback at a private school with a reputation to uphold. I was struggling to learn how to read and constantly getting into trouble. I would often mix my b's with my d's and at times skip over entire sentences when I would read out loud. One day, as we took a test, to my surprise I was one of the first to finish. I was so impressed by my work, but I didn't realize that the test had part two in the back. Of course, the teacher neglected to tell me, to teach me a lesson and failed me. My ADHD and overall behavior issues were perhaps even more apparent to the teachers, when a boy named Alejandro was bullying my friend Javier. I took matters into my own hands during recess. I approached him, he stayed quiet, I took his juice box, placed it inside his shirt, pressed it, causing his white polo to turn red and punched him in the face. Let's just say, he never bullied my friend again. Naturally, I ended up in the principal's office afterward, but that didn't stop me from enjoying my favorite after-school snack: a Coca-Cola ICEE and an empanadilla de pizza. I treated the rest of the day like any other. Standing up to a bully felt good, and I didn't really care what the adults had to say about it.

Even though they had plenty to say in the days that followed, the truth was, in order to meet their admissions quota, they couldn't afford to have kids like me held back, the so-called "troublemakers" who couldn't read. The other option was the public school system in Puerto Rico, which is not equipped to prepare their students for university life or their basic education needs. Their books are extremely outdated, and teachers barely live above the poverty line. As a result, they don't always show up to teach their classes because they're trying to make ends meet by balancing multiple jobs. This is probably why only eighteen percent of the island's population has a bachelor's degree. If parents can afford private school, they will make the financial commitment to send their children there. On the other hand, those who aren't as lucky can receive scholarships through a rigorous and extremely competitive process. Despite Puerto Rico having over 1,500 public schools and 500 private schools, only about six of the private schools are bilingual, which means that even though we are a commonwealth of the United States, most Puerto Ricans do not speak English fluently.

As I struggled through elementary school, my teachers kept insisting that therapy and ADHD medication would solve it all, basically saying "Take this damn pill, sit down and maybe you can stay here."

Academia San José was a Catholic school, the one my mother and aunt graduated from and where my brother attended. My grandparents were known in this school as well; they would volunteer to help the church that was part of this school, and they ran many fundraisers for them as well. Unfortunately, I was about to single-handedly destroy our family reputation in the school and the church. I wasn't meeting their educational expectations or behaving as they expected me to, so I had to pack all my belongings and find a new school.

Shortly after the student counselor spoke to my mother, I found myself enrolled in Parkville School, an expensive private school with a program to help children with learning disabilities. At ten years old, I carried what felt like a quiet sadness that I couldn't name or understand. I would begin to unravel and understand it many years later.

Circa 1996

My family couldn't afford it, but we tightened the purse strings, and my grandfather contributed significantly to give me this one and only opportunity. I met some great friends there, some whom I still keep in touch with today. The class was smaller to allow the teacher to be more dedicated to her students, and the pace was slower. The other students and I all had our differences like any other children, but I learned more during my time at that school than I ever had before. We were all misfits in our own ways, or at least a big part of the student body was, and somehow I found my tribe there. I still felt incomplete, but by playing basketball, talking about movies, the beach, and sharing similar cultural tastes, I finally had a safe space. The friendships I built in that school with MJ, Dre and others would carry for over 20 years. It was the best time of my academic career. It's as if life paused just enough for me to learn, to digest, to absorb the material. I even made it to the honor roll, despite still managing to get into trouble.

In eighth grade, I was part of an after-school program where we would do homework, eat a snack, and afterward play hoops and cards, or just talk until the parents picked us up. One day as I was talking to my friends and a teacher about homework, dreams and future plans, I mentioned that I wanted to do many things and eventually move to the U.S.

I mentioned how I loved to help animals and people. As I spoke passionately about my hopes for my future, my teacher said, "You have a good heart. Don't let the ugliness of the world take that away from you." I was surprised, but it left such a lasting impression that I still remember it to this day. A strange feeling washed over me, something I'd never experienced before—it was pride.

At that time in my life, no one was giving me positive reinforcement. It was all about how I needed to do better, be better, behave better, get better grades; how I needed to stay still and not get in trouble constantly. When others weren't saying those things, I was in a constant feedback loop of self-loathing. This recognition from someone else sparked a glimmer of hope in me that maybe I actually had potential, that I was good at something, and that my kind heart was something worth being proud of.

Unfortunately, that sense of hope was short-lived. The shame I carried only deepened as my father repeatedly called me stupid and that I wouldn't amount to anything. To this day, I don't think he knows I overheard him saying that to my mother during their phone calls.

In 2001, I was a freshman in high school, and let's just say my report card was more "F" than "A." I spent most of my time getting into trouble, whether it was skipping class or flipping the breakers off, because who wouldn't want a surprise day off?

In truth, I was on the verge of being expelled. One day, I heard my dad yelling at my mother over the phone about my grades and behavior. She gave me the phone and said, "It's your father. He wants to speak with you." Without skipping a beat, he yelled at me, "Out of all my children, you are the only one that is always giving me grief."

After months of building a reputation that didn't exactly work in my favor, I found myself playing hacky sack with friends after school. In an unfortunate moment, I lost control of the hacky sack and accidentally hit the principal. She turned around, said nothing, and quietly walked back to her office. A few days later, she informed my mother that I was on thin ice and suggested it might be time to consider a different school. At the time, mom was dating a man named Roy, another parental figure who seemed to have strong opinions about who I was, how I should be raised, and how to handle my "problematic" behaviors.

Roy was from Texas, working for an American-based company, and somehow ended up relocating to Puerto Rico for work. He had a commanding presence, was quick to anger, and wasn't exactly warm. His presence always made me feel uneasy. One afternoon, I came home to find him sitting with Mami in the living room. They had been discussing the recent conversation she'd had with the principal and what my options were moving forward. Roy raised his voice, suggesting that perhaps I should be expelled to "learn a lesson." I couldn't understand why he was even involved in this conversation. Without saying a word, I walked away mid-sentence and retreated to my room. To put it mildly, he was an asshole, emotionally abusive in fact. He was in my life for about two years until one day, he either disappeared or they broke up. Despite my attempts to resist, I felt utterly defeated, and the familiar cycle of self-doubt took over. It was as if I were swimming against the current. I couldn't express what I was feeling clearly, and even if I had, I doubted anyone would have taken the time to truly listen. Although I didn't want to leave and never got the chance to explain my side, I was removed from the school before I could make my case.

In retrospect, I can clearly see that I was in pain and acted that way because I didn't know how to reach out for help or how to find the root of that pain by myself. The pain was raw and undeniable, and the only escape I could find was to immerse myself completely in sports. It kept my mind constantly busy, and as I was very athletic, the stars somehow aligned. This worked for me until it didn't, and I ultimately ended up choosing other options to keep my mind busy.

After months of searching, my mother found a new school that I would later come to find, would take a toll on my mental health. My sense of tribe was abruptly taken from me, and I was put back in Catholic school, where I didn't feel safe, where my inner renegade would stay quiet just to fit in, just to survive.

By 2002, my sophomore year, that feeling of being broken, in pain, and lonely would have an even bigger impact than I ever thought possible. My dad was an avid golfer and would often participate in local golf tournaments. He had recently won one, and the prize was a two-night stay at a hotel. Since the hotel was near his home, he didn't have much use for it and gave me the prize instead, and I thought it would be a great way to spend my birthday. I held on tightly to this gift for months, barely able to contain my excitement. The location was near the beach, the hotel had a small pool, and a few restaurants within walking distance, and my mother agreed to chaperone us for the weekend. As my birthday was approaching, I was so excited to tell my new friends that we would do something fun and out of the ordinary. They agreed to come to the hotel for the weekend, but for some reason, rumors about me being gay started circulating around the school shortly after. The rumor was spread by one of the parents, and when it reached the others, they told their kids they couldn't attend my birthday. I felt crushed and heartbroken. I spent my birthday that year alone and ever since then, the only thing that I ever expect is a celebratory cake. I didn't know why people thought that about me. I wasn't even sure what I was feeling or who I was yet. The word *gay* had never even entered my mind. Was I confused? Yes. Did I know what I was feeling or thinking? Not really. How could someone else decide that for me? How could someone else tell me who I am?

In the aftermath, it felt like the only way to stop the pain and silence the rumors was to lie. So I pretended to have a crush on a boy from class. It worked. Over time the whispers faded. Fortunately I knew he was not interested in me he liked another girl which I was well aware of. I used that to my advantage. At that point I just needed a way to take back control of the narrative. I longed to figure out who I was for myself not because of what others told me. I remember going to the bathroom at school shortly after staring into the mirror and feeling nothing but hatred for the person looking back. I kept asking myself over and over What's is wrong with me?

My hurt, pain and confusion continued for many long months. The pain took over my mind, my body, my entire self. I felt that I had no control over anything, that my life was a lie day in and day out. It felt like I was trapped in an endless game of hide-and-seek—with myself and the world. The difference was, I was always the one hiding, and no one was ever looking for me.

One afternoon after school, I was home alone, nothing unusual. From the age of thirteen until I graduated high school, I was a latchkey kid. But on this particular day, something felt heavier. I found myself wondering what it would be like if I just didn't exist anymore. If I were gone, I thought, no more causing headaches for anyone, no more academic issues, no more behavioral problems, and the pain I carried might finally disappear. Thankfully, something stopped me midway, and instead, I stepped into the garage, got on my bike, and rode. I rode for hours, tears streaming down my face, trying to outpace the weight I was feeling. By the time I returned, my mother was home from my grandparents' house. She spent every afternoon there, caring for my grandmother, whose Alzheimer's was steadily getting worse.

A few months after my birthday, a new school year began, followed by winter break, and before I knew it, Valentine's Day was around the corner. In that time, I'd managed to shift the narrative about me just enough to breathe a little easier, but the rumors and questions never completely disappeared. Still, something was about to happen that would pull the spotlight away from me, at least for a while. In early February, I was in physical education class, just another typical day. However, for the past month or so, we had a new teacher, Mr. Ramirez. He had recently moved to Guaynabo from the other side of the island, where he had grown up and taught in a public school. He was in his late twenties, tall and fit, with glasses. He would not only teach the class in a fun and engaging way, but he also knew about food, music, and movies, the main topics that most teenagers will only talk about. He bonded with many of us, discussing the different up and coming bands on the island. I always carried my CD player in my backpack and would often listen to music as we walked back to school after P.E. Mr. Ramirez noticed me going through my CDs and realized we shared similar music tastes. The next class, he unexpectedly handed me a mixed CD, writing the band names with a black Sharpie for reference. I thanked him and went to class.

I didn't have a close group of friends at this school, but I often spoke to the same few people. One of them was Roberta, a girl who lived in my neighborhood, and we took the same bus home after school. On Valentine's Day, Roberta was proudly showing off the card her boyfriend had written for her, along with the flowers and chocolates he gave her. The card made its rounds through the classroom. When I read it, I realized I recognized the handwriting.

As the card continued circulating among my classmates, I grabbed my CD player, pulled out the CD, and stopped one of the girls just as she was about to hand the card to someone else. She looked at me, surprised. "What are you doing?" she asked.

I showed her the CD and said, "Do you think this is the same handwriting?"

She glanced at it, nodded, and asked, "Yeah… why?"

"This is Mr. Ramirez's handwriting," I told her. "It matches the writing on the card."

We both froze, stunned. Neither of us could believe it. After going back and forth about what to do, we couldn't decide whether I should speak to another teacher. From that moment on, P.E. class felt different. I became more and more suspicious of Mr. Ramirez and quietly cautioned the other girls to steer clear of him without offering too many details. Meanwhile, he had somehow managed to charm nearly everyone, especially those close to Roberta.

After months of worry, one afternoon, another teacher found Mr. Ramirez and Roberta making out in the back of the school.

He was fired on the spot. This triggered weeks of interviews for me and many of my classmates, with the Principal leading the sessions and notifying our parents. Many of the parents were in shock, struggling to believe that a predator had been allowed to teach at the school. I could hear their voices rising, accusations being thrown at the Principal, as we all waited outside her office.

I still don't know if the school failed to conduct a proper background check, but I later learned that Mr. Ramirez had been fired from the public school he worked at for what seemed to be the same reason. It wasn't until many years later, as an adult, that I realized he had been grooming us. He had manipulated everyone who had any kind of connection with Roberta, close friends, classmates, lab partners, and even me, someone who simply shared the bus with her every afternoon.

The groundwork he laid during that time had worked. We all thought he was the best teacher, and we spoke of him fondly around Roberta, which, in hindsight, was likely his ultimate goal. Apparently, he had obtained Roberta's phone number and home address. They would talk for hours on the phone, and he would visit her often when her parents weren't home. This all came to light during the investigation, as they spoke with neighbors as well.

Looking back, Roberta was raised by a single mother and was the oldest of three siblings. Her mother worked long hours to provide for their family, and when Roberta wasn't in school, she was at home taking care of her younger brothers. Roberta always sought to impress our class with elaborate stories. What she was really searching for through those stories was acceptance, attention, and love. As I got older, I couldn't help but feel sorry for her. Everyone seemed to be carrying their own burdens of pain.

What happened with Roberta made my news seem so small in a way, and put an end to the rumors. I still hated going to school, and the car ride every morning made my stomach twist in knots. I couldn't understand that feeling at the time. I couldn't even name it. I often skipped breakfast, afraid I'd get physically sick on the ride. For the rest of my high school years, I threw myself into basketball and weekends out, using them as a way to escape. It only clicked once I became an adult. It had been anxiety all along.

Despite my new found focus, I kept counting down the days until graduation, hoping that university would offer me some peace of mind and a safe space. In 2004, I graduated, and it was then that I began to truly understand what it meant to grow up on an island where Catholicism was the dominant religion. As I started to slowly come to terms with who I was, it felt like I had to live in constant fear. Some people around me couldn't understand me, and their faith led them to view the LGBT community as something to harm, which in turn meant harming me. I never chose to be this way. This is not a choice. Who would willingly choose to live in the shadows, never trusting anyone, always looking over their shoulder?

To this day, I still struggle with the adoption of the word "queer" by the LGBT community. The idea behind it is that the community reclaimed a term once used as an insult, turning it into a symbol of empowerment. Yet, the root of the word has always meant something strange or odd, and I don't consider myself odd. I don't want, nor need, to stand out because of who I love or who I married.

That said, I consider myself fortunate to have never experienced personal harm because of who I am and who I love. Sadly, I know of friends and acquaintances who were not so lucky.

In 2009, Jorge Steven Lopez Mercado was brutally murdered. The killer approached him as he walked near a club by seemingly being interested. He invited Jorge out and drove up to a mountain near the middle of the island. Once they arrived, after the killer had manipulated the entire situation, he tortured Jorge, decapitated and dismembered him, then partially burned the body. He walked away and abandoned what was left of Jorge in the mountains for law enforcement to find. The LGBT community in Puerto Rico was small at the time. We all knew or heard of Jorge.

In court, the man who took Jorge's life claimed he panicked upon realizing Jorge was gay. He relied on what is known as the "gay panic" defense, a legal argument that attempts to excuse violence by blaming it on fear or discomfort with someone's identity. It is a defense rooted in bias, used far too often to justify what can never truly be justified. Across the country, outrage has grown over how this tactic dehumanizes victims and reinforces harmful stereotypes. As of 2025, some states have banned its use, but in many places, it still has not been fully erased from the system. In Jorge's case, the court rejected the defense. The pain inflicted could not be undone or reasoned away. The man who killed him was found guilty and sentenced to 99 years in prison.

For all of us, if you weren't killed on the island for being gay, you were probably battling severe depression because of it, braving a tug-of-war between your authentic self and a different version of yourself that could more easily find a place in the world. You had to be very good at hiding the pain, hiding who you were. As it goes, some of us got really good at this. Others, not so much. For some, the burden of their depression was too overwhelming to bear, and it tragically cost them their lives. This was between 2004 and 2010, a time when legal protections for the LGBT community were scarce, and the world felt much harsher for us.

Back then, I had a friend named Cyntia who went to university with me. On the surface, she seemed happy. She played pool at the local bar, joined us at the beach, sat through lectures, and showed up for our late night study sessions. She did all the things you'd expect from a typical university student. But there was something else, something quieter. Whenever we ended up at the bar, she'd head straight for the jukebox and spend a few dollars to play "Niña" by La 5ta Estación. The song told the story of a girl weighed down by pain, a girl without dreams, who smiled for no reason and saw only sorrow in the world around her. The final line always lingered: "Con su vida no querrá continuar"—With her life, she will not want to go on. It always intrigued me, her quiet attachment to the song, and how she never explained why.

A few semesters later, on a Thursday night, I went to the Eros Club with a friend. It was one of those rare places where you could be completely, unapologetically yourself. I remember standing near the bar, next to one of those tall black round tables, chatting about a class project I was very intentionally putting off.

Jose asked, "Wait, when is it due? Are we out of time?"

"Pretty sure it's tomorrow afternoon," I said.

He raised an eyebrow. "Then maybe we should think about heading out soon?"

I laughed. "Yeah… probably."

In the middle of our conversation, Cynthia walked up and asked how our night was going. She said she would be heading out soon, then leaned in and hugged me tightly, something she rarely did. "It was really nice to see you. You're such a great person, Marita," she said softly.

As she walked away, something felt off, but I couldn't quite put my finger on it. Cynthia was never one to show much emotion, so the unexpected hug caught me off guard. Still, I shrugged it off. Eventually, we wrapped up the night, and I drove home like I had so many times before.

As I walked into class the next day, I saw that the classmate that had initially introduced me to Cynthia was crying. I asked him, "What's wrong?" He wiped his eyes, struggling to speak. With halting breaths and peppered silences, he finally said, "Cynthia took her own life last night." The words struck me like a punch to the chest. A single thought echoed in my mind: Was I the last person to see her alive? Should I have noticed something? Should I have said more, done more? Later that afternoon, as we gathered for lunch, someone shared that she had left a note for her parents. Just one line from it clung to my memory, sharp and heavy: "I cannot go on."

For weeks, guilt followed me. I kept asking our group of friends, how did we miss it? She'd play that one song over and over. That had to mean something, didn't it? Jennifer, one of her closest friends, finally broke the silence. "I tried to help her," she said "I even spoke to her mom a few times. There was nothing more we could have done." I really wanted to believe her, but I still felt so much guilt.

I knew exactly how she felt. I had felt the same way for years. In time we all moved on, with classes, with life, but the memory of Cynthia's passing stayed with me.

What happened to Jorge, and what Cynthia went through, only deepened the weight I was already carrying. As time went on, I couldn't shake the feeling that I was broken, like there was something inside of me that needed fixing. It felt as though anyone walking past me on a crowded street could see it, that they could somehow sense the emptiness inside me, the hole in my chest that begged to be filled.

For years, I carried the heavy burden of society's expectations, this idea of what "normal" should look like. And of course, all that pressure only made things worse. I found myself stuck in a never-ending cycle of pain, struggling through my teenage years and into my early twenties, searching for something, for anything to heal.

Embarking in My Twenties

As I went through my university years, the checklist that had been handed down to me by society, my friends, and my family remained firmly in place, shaping many of my choices. I never truly felt like I had real options in life, so I continued to follow the checklist, hoping that somehow, things would magically improve. In the midst of it all, I found comfort not only in adrenaline fueled escapades, parties, and nights of drinking, but also in writing. At the time, I didn't fully understand it, but looking back,

I see that it was another piece of the system I had unknowingly built for myself. Writing became my way of processing, my outlet for sharing my thoughts. When I revisited those old notebooks, though, I couldn't help but notice how much of it was written under the influence. Perhaps I should've written a comedy book instead? A missed opportunity, next time. Humor was my go-to friend whenever I didn't know what else to say or do.

On the other hand, adrenaline was a constant companion during this time of my life, especially through bodysurfing. The rush of those waves at Puerto Rico's most dangerous beaches was exhilarating. My older brother, Mario Jr., introduced me to it. He and his friends would go every weekend, but I was always too young to join them. Growing up, my relationship with him was defined by our eleven-year age gap. As a kid, I looked up to him, as most younger siblings do. I wanted to mimic his every move. I wanted to play the sports he played and listen to the music he listened to. But as I grew older, our connection began to fade.

He met Viviana shortly after college, though technically they'd known of each other during those years. It wasn't until they ended working together that some well-meaning cowork-ers set them up on a blind date that their paths truly crossed and something just clicked. Viviana is the kind of woman who doesn't just enter your life, she anchors it. That's exactly what she did for him. She grounded him in a way no one else ever had. And when their two boys were born, she quietly became the steady force at the center of their growing family, calm, capable, and headstrong.

Once he got married, the distance between us grew even more. It was during this time that I began to truly understand the complexities of expectations. I had imagined that my older brother would always be there, offering advice, sharing a drink, leaning on each other as we grew. But the reality is, we can't control the evolution of family relationships. They shift and change, as we do. And why wouldn't they? We're all constantly evolving. I don't blame him for us growing apart, for marrying and starting his own family. He needed that, I think. His family became his refuge, just as, in time, when I built a family of my own, it became mine.

I love my nephews, too. Simon possesses a quiet kind of brilliance, the kind that doesn't need to announce itself. He listens carefully before he speaks, and when he does, his words carry a thoughtfulness well beyond his years. There's a calm, steady kindness in him that never seeks the spotlight but is always felt. He was born in 2004, just as I was entering college, and I've watched him grow from a quiet baby into a young man who, in so many ways, is a reflection of Mario Jr., not just in appearance but in spirit.

Finn was born in 2009, and from the very beginning, it was clear he wasn't going to blend into the background. He's loud in the best way, full of energy, humor, and the kind of charisma that fills a room before he even says a word. In a family that's seen all kinds of personalities, Finn reminds me most of myself. There's a spark in him, a boldness, and a way of turning every conversation into either a joke or a pitch. What sets him apart, even at a young age, is his natural acumen for business. He's the kind of kid who doesn't just want to sell lemonade, he's figuring out how to scale the stand, cut costs, and track his profits.

Those two boys make me laugh and help me understand the love that one can have for children.

I'm learning how to let go of my attachment to how I want things to be. Better to let things flow naturally, as relationships do. I strongly believe we create images of how these relationships should be in our minds. We create expectations because we like to envision the future, and we start to believe those images will become a reality. In truth, we don't know how things will evolve. As you may have heard before, sometimes relationships are for a reason, a season, or a lifetime. As unpredictable as life is, we never know which one it will be.

I have two brothers: Mario Jr., my older brother, and Sam, my younger brother. My older brother Mario Jr. is a quiet, thoughtful presence, shy and reserved but undeniably sharp. Though he doesn't seek the spotlight in conversation, his intelligence shines through in everything he does. Despite his calm demeanor, he has a deep love for sports like soccer, frisbee, and bodysurfing. These activities bring out a more relaxed and playful side of him, where he connects easily with others. He also has a creative side; he used to draw when he was younger and later learned to play the drums in adulthood. It's in these moments, whether on the field, in the waves, or behind his drum kit, that you see the full measure of who he is. When I was about twelve or thirteen, he would go out with friends and come home late. I waited for him impatiently, and as soon as he got home, we'd head to the kitchen for cereal, Corn Flakes with milk in our bowls. Then we'd go to his room, where a small TV sat on a dresser, and watch Comedy Central until our bowls were empty. "Alright, time for bed," he'd say, and I'd head across the hall to my room and fall asleep. It became our weekend ritual, a quiet way to hang out while Mom was sleeping.

My younger brother Sam was born when I was eleven during my father's second marriage. People warned me I'd be jealous after all I had been the youngest for so long but to my surprise Sam and I became inseparable. I taught him how to shave, how to dress, tie a tie, talk to girls, and even how to manage his money. I gave him his first beer and explained the idea of "luck" at the casino, really just how to look for odds and percentages when playing roulette. I saw these things as essentials, lessons on how to enjoy life without taking it too seriously. I cared about him so much. In a way, I was trying to be the older sibling I had longed for myself, a cool, sophisticated older sibling I could learn from. At the time, my new stepmother was only a few years older than my older brother. In fact, they attended university at the same time, which unsurprisingly didn't sit well with Mario Jr. But from my perspective as the much younger sibling, she came across as fun and friendly. She welcomed me when I visited, encouraged me to spend time with Sam, and even called to check in on me when dad didn't. If I needed something like a new backpack for school, she'd buy it before dad had a chance to say no.

But as I got older, things shifted. She wasn't as warm or open anymore. Looking back, I realize that throughout my life, I've had many different parental figures and somehow, it always felt like I ended up disappointing each of them in the end.

When I was young, long before my father remarried and Sam was born, our family would go on trips to the beach several times a year. It was always just the three of us: Mom, Mario Jr., and me.

The more we visited, the more I wanted to learn to bodysurf, and eventually, Mario Jr. started teaching me the basics. As I got more into the sport, his old surfboard became mine to use.

One day, on a beach trip, I decided to bodysurf with my brand-new glasses, the same pair my mom had bought me just a week before. She was too busy reading to notice me heading out, and once I was in the water, waiting for the perfect wave, I glanced over at Mario Jr. for guidance. Following his instructions, I caught the wave that came, but it took me and my glasses down. Naturally, I lost them.

When I told my mom, she was furious. She made us clean up everything and head back to the car. I could see the anger and disappointment in her eyes. Growing up, things were tight at times. My dad paid child support, but we still had to make it stretch. As we walked to the car, I spotted a kebab cart and asked if we could get one before heading home. She snapped, "A kebab! No, you get zero kebabs. We're going home, and I'll make you a fra-fra-fra!" To this day, I still ask her, "Mom, what's a fra-fra-fra?" She laughs and says, "I was so angry I couldn't think of anything, I didn't even know what I wanted to say." It's hilarious now, and the story has become a cherished family story.

In hindsight, this one trip, this one weekend adventure was how my love for bodysurfing began. As I aged, my love for the beach and bodysurfing grew. I would be at the beach almost every Sunday, rain or sunshine. Even more so if it rained because that meant that I could catch the biggest waves.

In the water, I was in the zone, literally. I was mostly in the swash zone, the zone of wave action that moves as tides come in and out. Once I saw the perfect wave form, I would start paddling to make sure I wouldn't miss it. That's where the adrenaline kicks in, as the wave slowly picks you up. It was a race to the frothy, bubbly surf zone. I quickly became addicted to the whole experience, the rush that you get when you finally catch the perfect wave. I started to bodysurf even more during and after hurricanes. You know, when they have the red flags all over the beach that clearly tell you not to get into the water. No, seriously. It was hard to explain it back then, but now I can see it all clearly. I needed an anchor, a home, a place of refuge, something to use in my life when things didn't seem to make sense.

We all experience this. It's why some people take on running or baking later in life. We are all looking for that anchor, that place for when we don't know where to turn, that place that's ours alone that we can come to as we are.

As I continued bodysurfing, I kept putting myself in danger until I reached a point where I thought I was unstoppable. I believed it so much that one day in my freshman year in college, I had the scariest near-death experience. My friend Georgia and I decided to do a road trip to Mayaguez, which was on the other side of the island. Our friend Claire was going to school in that town. We all had graduated from high school together but ended up in different universities all across the island.

After about two hours of driving, we finally reached Mayaguez. I know it might not seem like much of a road trip to folks in the U.S., but Puerto Rico is only 110 miles long, so for us, it felt like quite the adventure. Once we arrived, we spent the first night barhopping, starting the night at El Garabato, a popular college bar in Mayaguez, enjoying the low-80s weather and reminiscing about our high school days. We cheered for the weekend with shots and met Claire's new college friends. The next morning, we decided to head to Rincon, a neighboring town known for its popular beaches, where we could relax for the day. I didn't bring my board on this trip. I had a group of friends who would body-surf, but Georgia and Claire weren't part of it. Instead, Claire and I decided to go swim, while Georgia read and listened to music on the shore.

At the time, we didn't realize how strong the current was. Even though the waves looked small from the shore, the current could still be powerful, even when there weren't big waves rolling in. This beach had hosted several professional surfing competitions, yet we still decided to go in. Some might call it naive; others might say we were misinformed. Now, I just call it plain stupidity. My love for the ocean ran so deep that I believed I was always in full control. The water that day was just perfect, not cold, and the gentle summer breeze made for the perfect beach day. As we walked into the water, we continued to catch up on life, laughing and discussing how the transition from high school to college was going, the uncertainty, the novelty, and the excitement of it all. Not long after that, we realized how far away from the shore we were. Initially, we didn't panic. We just thought we'd gotten carried away by the water, the waves, and the conversation. We tried to swim back, but the current kept pulling us out farther. This time, we became slightly concerned. We tried once more to swim back to shore, but the more we tried the farther back the waves took us.

The situation began to escalate quickly. As Claire's panic grew, a sense of urgency took hold of me. I started to think through our options, carefully weighing what we could do out there in the middle of the ocean. The beach was deserted that day. No one was around to hear us if we screamed for help. The current was too strong and still pulling us farther and farther from the shore. As I looked everywhere, I noticed the reef as a viable option. As a last resort, I decided we should swim to the reef and allow the waves to take us close enough to pull our bodies up and away from danger. I believed that if we swam to our left, in a horizontal direction, we could make it somewhere instead of waiting in the middle of the open water. At nineteen, I was in my prime. I was extremely athletic, so I knew we could make it out safe. Even though it didn't seem like the best idea, it was the only option we had at the time. We swam toward a light-brown coral reef. From a distance it looked small, but it was long enough that if we successfully climbed it and walked all the way to the end, it would leave us by the shore, just a few steps away from Georgia. As we inched closer and closer, I noticed the reef was actually big and mostly above water. This was going to be extremely helpful for my strategy to just let the ocean do the work and lift us back to safety.

As we got closer, I told her, "Brace yourself. Use all your strength to climb the reef."

She hesitated, her voice trembling. "What if I can't, Marita? What if I can't hold on?"

"I've got you," I said, my voice steady despite the chaos. "We'll make it. We have to survive."

But even as the words left my mouth, doubt ate away at me. The thought that we might not make it out alive was too much to bear. I don't remember how I climbed the reef, but I do remember resisting the pain in my hands. I dug my nails into that reef and, with the help of the waves, lifted my body up. I knew I was bleeding, but I also knew this was my only option for survival.

Once I was standing on the reef, I took stock of my body and found not one scar. Aside from my bloody hands and broken nails, I was totally fine. I couldn't believe I was safely out of the water and out of immediate danger.

As I was standing on the reef, I turned to look for Claire. She was nowhere to be found. I called out her name at the top of my lungs, terrified for her safety. I took a cautious step forward, straining to catch a glimpse of her through the waves. In the blink of an eye, a massive wave slammed into me, pulling me under once more. For what felt like an eternity, the waves tossed me violently against the reef, their force relentless and unyielding. I was fighting to survive with every bit of strength I had, but I was running out of air. I remember staring up at the sunlight filtering through the water, thinking that this was it, that it would be the last thing I ever saw. My mind drifted to my family and the heartbreak they would endure if I didn't make it back. Exhausted, I stopped fighting the ocean, resigned to whatever would come next. I still remember my eyes growing heavy, slowly closing as I began to drift out of consciousness. Just as I gave in, a massive wave surged beneath me, pushing me to the surface. Suddenly, I was able to take a breath again. I climbed the reef once more with what could only be described as a burst of adrenaline. I started to cough up water and held my chest, taking a minute to fully catch my breath. Once I was up on the reef again, I realized that this time I was bleeding all over my body. I had battled with the reef, and it was obvious that the reef won the round.

As I looked to the shore, I saw Claire had been rescued by a surfer who we later found out was named Steve. He was visiting from the US to experience the Puerto Rican surfer lifestyle. Steve the surfer came back and said, "Jump back in the water, and we can swim to shore with my board."

I was too scared to jump back in. I asked, "Can you bring me shoes? I would rather walk from the reef to the shore" As I waited for him to arrive, I looked around at the blood dripping from my body and at the sea cockroaches on the reef. It was quiet, I could only hear the waves and the whales as I saw them from a distance. When he came back with my shoes, he saw me bleeding and said, "You will probably need to go to the hospital." That was the understatement of the century. Before long, my shoes were covered in blood, my hands were shaking, and I was in shock.

As we reached the shore, both Claire and Georgia hugged me. We couldn't believe what had just happened. Georgia had no idea that we had almost drowned; she didn't even realize that anything had happened. However, a group of tourists saw the whole thing from afar. As it turns out, they were visiting a lighthouse, and from there they'd seen everything and called 911. As we collected our belongings, an ambulance and a news truck pulled up. The EMTs wanted to take us to the hospital, but I was hesitant about the reporters coming toward us with a camera. If this made the local news, it would just give my mother another reason to complain about how reckless I was. Claire and I hurried up to the ambulance, and Georgia drove my car behind us. Of course, the accident still made the news that evening. To my surprise, my mother didn't see it.

I learned during the drive to the hospital that during the winter in Rincon, whales will come close enough to the shore that you can see them from the lighthouse. I didn't realize it, but I had been only thirty feet from those beautiful creatures. For some reason, sometime after the accident, I felt driven to research why they were making loud noises as we struggled in the water.

After reading several articles, I discovered that whales are capable of experiencing a wide range of emotions. To this day, I like to believe that they were calling out for help, sensing our desperation and wanting to save us. I genuinely feel they were showing empathy toward us.

When we arrived at the hospital, I was told that seventy percent of my body had lacerations from the reef. They had to clean every single cut on me. It was excruciating. They had to scrape, clean, and move on to the next one. The scars have mostly faded, but there's one on my right shoulder that still has a bit of depth to it. It's small and thin, yet it serves as a constant reminder of the second chance I've been given to keep living.

When the hospital called, my mother couldn't believe the story and was hesitant to proceed with any approvals or paperwork. It took hours of convincing before she finally agreed. As we sat in the hospital waiting, a woman approached and asked what had happened. After I explained in detail, she told me, "You're lucky. My husband, a devoted surfer, passed away on that same beach eight years ago."

That night, we stayed in Claire's dorm room before heading back home the next day. With all my bruises, I was unable to drive my car, so Georgia drove us back. When we arrived home, my mom didn't say anything. She just hugged me and hid my bodyboard in case I was thinking of ever going back to the beach. I was traumatized for months and couldn't go near the ocean for a long time. Even the sound of the waves was enough to trigger me. Nightmares of drowning haunted me, and to this day, I can't watch a movie with a drowning scene.

You might be thinking that this is where my journey to stillness begins, but no. I eventually made peace with what happened and ten months later visited that same beach with a friend. I stood there, looking into the horizon as a tear ran down my face. I felt embarrassed and guilty for making such a stupid decision. I had made one poor decision after the other, some that could have actually cost me my life. I collected some sand from the beach in a small jar and never used a bodyboard again.

Over time I found comfort in drinking and other adrenaline-seeking adventures. These were dangerous too, but none of them brought me as close to death as that one time. I jumped from waterfalls around the island, competed in street races and drank at least four days a week. As I write this, all the memories and feelings are coming back to me.

I always believed I relied on these high-risk adventures to cope with the toughest parts of my life, but looking back, it started much earlier. The only way I knew to deal with the emptiness, the unfulfillment, and the shame of who I was, was by diving into reckless adventures.

The thrill of those adventures distracted me, taking my mind to another place. It took years of introspection to piece it all together, to understand what was really driving me toward these self-destructive behaviors. The novelty of those adventures kept my mind busy and took me to another place.

Life in Puerto Rico was incredibly fun, but as I grew older, I began to question whether the environment I had been raised in had paved the way for all my reckless adventures. The constant, unsettling feeling of searching for something more seemed to overshadow everything. After spending a year wrestling with these thoughts following my accident on the beach, I finally found the courage to start stepping into the person I wanted to be, I decided to come out to a few people, beginning with my two oldest friends. We'd known each other since we were ten, so it felt like the safest place to start.

They took it well. As I told them, it was as if they had always known but had never asked about it. They'd allowed me the space to figure it out and piece it together on my own. One day as we spent the afternoon on the patio of one of their houses, one of my friends wanted me to open a MySpace account. Remember MySpace, kids? At that time, you could add your sexual orientation to your profile, and my friend ended up opening the account for me and, of course, selected lesbian without checking with me first. I didn't log in for days, completely unaware of what was happening, but to my surprise, text messages and calls with questions started to trickle in.

After the news broke, both Claire and Georgia stopped talking to me, along with several other friends. I was devastated and so ashamed of who I was that this just fed my destructive behaviors even more. This only led me to ruminating over the fact that I had risked my safety, my life, to save Claire, yet all it took was finding out that I was gay to never speak to me again. I could not understand how she could turn her back on someone simply for being gay, for simply being who they are.

Since Puerto Rico is such a small island, we still ran into each other at local bars. But even then, Claire never spoke to me again. Georgia and I crossed paths a little more often, and one night, after four years of silence, she apologized over a few drinks at a local bar. We hugged, and slowly, we began to rebuild our friendship. In fact, it was so repaired that we ended up sharing an apartment for almost a year in our early twenties. We supported each other through young adulthood, trying to build careers, surviving breakups, and navigating first dates. She was even there the day I decided to completely change my life and buy a one-way ticket to San Francisco. She never questioned it, almost as if she knew I could do anything I set my mind to. Before I left, she wrote me a letter filled with hope, inspiration, and love, encouraging my dreams and my decision.

Years later, she was there at my wedding. But don't worry, we'll get to that part.

The Edge of the Cliff

I struggled through most of my university years, failing classes more times than I can count. I only attended four sessions of the same class, and on the last day of the semester in my sophomore year, the teacher looked at me and asked, "Who are you?" I didn't really care and took it all as a joke. Even though I was struggling with my classes, I had become sort of a stud with the girls shortly after coming out. I would cruise the campus in my red-pearl Mitsubishi Lancer ES, and I spent most of my paychecks on it by adding a bar in the trunk, a DVD player in the backseat, and a state-of-the-art sound system. Once you heard the classic hot-rod "Ooga Ahooga" horn that I installed in the car, you knew it was me turning the corner.

Circa 2005

As dating was something new to me, I didn't skip a beat to take it all in. I dated many women, my charm, natural masculine energy, and comedic timing made dinner dates a breeze for me. My clever pickup lines came naturally. I was finally taking life in, feeling I was free, as it should be rather than hiding behind an unwanted mask.

Toward the end of junior year, this stud met a girl named Lisa. We started dating, going to dinners and gatherings with friends, and taking afternoon walks where we would eat ice cream. Before long, we became exclusive, and our conversations went on for hours. She seemed to be driven by the idea of being together, which was unnerving, but I tried not to overthink it. For the first time in my life, someone was only focusing on highlighting the fun and positive things I had to offer. All this happened out of nowhere, as I was juggling feeling overwhelmed with the pressure of college, work, and thinking about what to do with my future. We dated for many months and met each other's friends and family. I had dated many other women at this point but had never had a relationship last this long.

One day while I was driving, she suddenly asked, "What if I moved in?"

I heard her clearly but still replied, a bit unsure, "With me?"

She smiled and said, "Yes, of course."

I hesitated, caught off guard. But before I could even respond, she added, "My lease is up soon, and this just makes sense, we already spend most, if not all, of our time together."

I nodded and without much more discussion, said yes.

By the time we moved in together, I had a full-time job and had changed my schedule to take classes at night. Just like that, my destructive behaviors, still very much alive, took a back seat. With over twelve credits per semester, a job, and a live-in girlfriend, I didn't have the time to do or think about much else. My life wasn't exactly glamorous, but it felt like a step in the right direction. Things seem to be going well. The relationship helped me grow, requiring me to be more responsible as we lived together. It was the first time I had fallen truly in love, or so I thought at the time.

Even though things were going well, I still battled constantly with who I was and what I wanted out of life. I still felt unheard, lost, alone, and hopeless. With effort, I managed to push it all aside and we continued to live our life together. I didn't want to lose her, and I put so much effort into keeping the relationship together that I ended up losing sight of myself.

After nearly three years together, something began to shift. Lisa started to pull away, and it felt like we were living on two separate islands under the same roof. I tried checking in with her multiple times, asking if something was wrong, but she always gave the same answer: "Things are okay. We're okay."

There was never a clear moment to press further. We hadn't had any major fights or blowouts that would naturally lead to a deeper conversation. Sure, we argued from time to time like any couple, but nothing that ever felt like it could end us.

Still, I began to notice changes. She started spending more time at her mom's house, not just on weekends but during the week too. At home, she became fixated on her closet, constantly cleaning it out, sorting through old clothes.

One day, while she was mid-organization, I finally asked, "Why are you always going through your clothes?"

She replied, "I'm making room for new stuff and just figuring out what I want to leave at my mom's or donate."

It seemed harmless enough at the time. But something about it didn't sit right.

I didn't know it at the time, but I was standing on the edge of the cliff, and the ground underneath me was slowly crumbling. One Tuesday, as I pulled into the parking lot of our apartment, I noticed Lisa's car wasn't there. Immediately, something felt off. We had our routine down to the minute. I knew exactly when she'd be home. I opened the front door and stepped into silence. The apartment was half-empty. Drawers were open, shelves cleared, and on the kitchen table sat a note. She was gone. There wasn't much explanation, just that she'd realized she wanted a family, and couldn't see that future with a woman. My heart dropped.

Panic set in. My mind spun with questions, confusion, and a wave of emotions I couldn't untangle. I stood frozen, then slowly sank to the floor, my back against the wall. Shame crept in like an old familiar shadow. I was flooded with memories of friends who stopped talking to me when I came out, of my father's distant disappointed stare, as if I were a problem he didn't know how to solve. In that moment, it felt like the universe was confirming my deepest fear—that no matter how hard I tried, nothing would ever truly change. That maybe I was destined to fall short, to never quite be enough. I called my mother, but my voice was so shaky I could barely get the words out. I ended up staying at her house for a week. The silence in my apartment was just too much to bear. It felt like I was stuck in a cycle of bad decisions, each one followed by regret and shame. What once felt like the right choice always seemed to unravel into another painful lesson. At night, I'd lie in bed staring at the ceiling, the quiet pressing in on me. I kept asking myself: Why did this have to happen? What did I do wrong?

Why could I never be good enough? The self-loathing train had arrived at its station, and I was caught up in the "All aboard!"

For months, I struggled, pushing through, hoping things would get better. That had always been my go-to solution, just power through. But I felt like I was losing control of my life. The pressure of a full-time job and the weight of being a full-time student taking night classes felt overwhelming.

So, I reached out to my childhood psychologist. She wrote a note for my manager, explaining that I was battling constant panic attacks and struggling to focus on anything. There were times when I'd be driving and suddenly, at a stoplight, my heart would race, my hands would sweat, and I'd start hyperventilating to the point where I had to pull over and collect myself.

When I handed the doctor's note to my manager, I could see the doubt in her eyes. To her, it seemed like I was just looking for an extended vacation. She wasn't eager to grant the time off, but after some back-and-forth, she reluctantly agreed to three weeks, even though the doctor had recommended four. I knew, though, that if I didn't come back after that, I'd be out of a job.

For the first time in my life, I allowed myself some grace. Most of my life, I feared appearing weak, thinking I wouldn't survive if people saw my struggles. I convinced myself that showing weakness would be the perfect excuse to lose the little self-confidence I had left. During those three weeks, I went to a few classes and drank way too much. I didn't use the time as wisely as I had planned. I was struggling in every area of my life, and I wasn't being kind to myself. While I had given myself permission to heal, I was rushing through the process. At times, I've been my own worst enemy, and this period really emphasized that. One weekend, while walking through the mall with friends after lunch, we stopped by a bookstore. As I browsed the shelves, one book cover caught my eye. It was *The Accidental Billionaires: The Founding of Facebook* by Ben Mezrich.

This was an older copy of the book, that was adapted by Aaron Sorkin for the 2010 film *The Social Network*. You have to remember this was 2012. Facebook was barely scratching the surface, and social media and it's founders had yet to become a big dilemma. This company was the catalyst for more social media companies. After MySpace and Friendster, Facebook combined elements of both into one and gave us the ultimate social media platform at the tip of our fingers. As I read the book, I was immediately hooked by how the story unfolded. This book had an edge, the book drew me in and I wanted to learn all I could from it. That life, the one they all had, seemed like something so out of reach for me. I never imagined I'd be a part of the tech startup world, surrounded by so much creativity and energy.

At the time, all I could see was Mark Zuckerberg's unwavering determination, something I had never felt about anything in my own life. I started comparing his journey to mine, but not because I wanted to live his life. I was trying to figure out how I could position myself to feel the kind of passion and determination about my work, career or whatever I decided to do. I had never felt that way about any of my own dreams, probably because they weren't truly my dreams. I was chasing what others thought was success, not what I truly wanted. That book sparked a fire in me to seek discomfort, to step outside of my comfort zone, and to truly feel alive like I could dream bigger. It was a pivotal moment in my life, the first time I felt I could pause my checklist and take a new direction, one that really made me feel alive and excited. I realized I needed to see what the world beyond Puerto Rico had to offer.

This one book created a ripple effect leading to a new chapter of my life. As I read, I highlighted the different coding languages that Mark Zuckerberg mentioned so I could learn more about them later on. I highlighted places, languages, and classes, and after I was done, I researched them for hours. Once I finished the book, I started to examine every aspect of my life and think of all the possibilities. I had a dead-end job, I struggled through my classes, but at the same time, I was almost done with my bachelor's degree. I had my heart broken, and I felt so lost and worthless. Would I ever find a job that I was good at? Would I ever be happy? I was still in university with a small savings account, so I couldn't do much of anything, or at least it didn't feel like I had many options.

Then I did what anyone else would have done in my position: I started to Google what I could do. As I started deep-diving, internship programs began to pop up. In the end, I found one I was interested in, located in San Francisco. The process consisted of me submitting some initial paperwork, followed by some interviews, a portfolio review, and waiting to see if I had been accepted. I thought, why not? What do I have to lose? I didn't have a coding portfolio, but I could start creating one as best as I could.

After months of waiting anxiously, I finally received the call on a Tuesday morning. I had been accepted. Suddenly, it was real. Suddenly, it was real. Now came the harder part: telling my family I was leaving for a two-month internship that didn't guarantee a job at the end. As much as I wanted to get the internship, I never thought I'd be successful. I barely told anyone about the opportunity because I didn't want anyone to tell me to skip it or that I couldn't do it. I knew I needed this opportunity more than anything. My family was supportive of my decision to take the internship, but at the same time, they couldn't help but question why I was leaving. To them, it felt like I was running away from them, from the island, from the life I knew. In reality, I was the only one from my immediate family that had ever ventured away from Puerto Rico.

New Hope

As I packed my two suitcases and finalized the details of my departure, word somehow reached my ex-girlfriend Lisa that I was leaving. She reached out, wanting to meet. That time in my life is a bit of a blur, probably because I was so consumed by the excitement of the new chapter ahead, but I agreed to a conversation, thinking maybe it would bring some closure.

We ended up speaking over the phone. She told me her life hadn't been the same and said she'd love to visit me in San Francisco. I didn't hesitate. I told her no. I went further and said I probably wouldn't be coming back to live in Puerto Rico permanently. I needed a clean break, a fresh start. I wanted to build a future and a family of my own, something she hadn't envisioned with me when we were together.

She mentioned the possibility of transferring her job to San Francisco, but again, I said no. It was time for both of us to move on. She hadn't believed in me when it mattered, and I was done holding onto something that no longer served me. Out of frustration, she snapped, "I'll see you when you come back home, back to Puerto Rico!"

A few weeks later, it was time to leave. I boarded a plane from San Juan to San Francisco, nervous about the uncertainty that lay ahead. I had never been farther than Florida, and even then, it was just to visit extended family. But this was different. I needed to make a mark, to spark a wave of change in my life. It was time to start living with intention.

As the plane touched down in San Francisco, doubt crept in. Had I made a mistake? I couldn't shake the questions running through my mind, especially given my track record of poor decisions. I had no backup plan. This *was* the plan. Only later in life would I come to understand the importance of having a contingency plan.

Walking through the airport, I was sweating like a snowman in the sun, not just from the physical effort of navigating the terminal, but from the weight of everything I was carrying emotionally. After locating baggage claim and retrieving my luggage, I grabbed a cab and headed toward my new address. When we finally pulled into the city, I checked in with the internship team and rushed upstairs to my assigned room. My roommate hadn't arrived yet, so I claimed the better bed and started unpacking, still trying to wrap my head around everything that was unfolding.

Those two months in San Francisco were everything I had hoped for. While I struggled with some of my coding projects, my determination and the extra hours I put in at night helped me push through. Sixty days, that's all the time I had to turn this opportunity into lasting change. My role focused on front-end development for an early-stage tech startup dedicated to optimizing online interactions for major brands.

The office was tucked away on Pine Street near the Financial District, while I was living on Mission Street. Each morning, I took the Muni to Montgomery Street and walked the rest of the way. Life in San Francisco was a world apart from Puerto Rico, but I embraced the change and found myself enjoying the rhythm of city living.

The startup office itself was modest, small, slightly musty, and full of character. The elevator barely fit three people, and the floors were a mix of worn wood and faded green carpet. The bathroom felt more like a converted broom closet. The company was run by three founders who kept things lean. Their version of office perks? A coffee machine, a couple of cracked leather couches that practically swallowed you whole, and a few scattered desks.

To break up the long hours in front of our screens, they had a couple of golf clubs, some golf balls, and a cup set up for impromptu putting practice. It wasn't much, but it quickly grew on me. Before I knew it, I was enjoying golf more than I ever anticipated; it became the only real escape from the stiff chairs and the creaky twenty-dollar desks we all worked at.

The three founders each had distinct personalities, backgrounds, and management styles, but their differences somehow united them in running the business. The CEO, Jeff, was a quiet man who only showed emotion when the company was doing well or when someone helped him out. Most days, you'd find him tucked away in his office, which held little more than a desk, a laptop, and dim lighting. He wasn't very personable, but I kept devising a strategy to approach him before my internship ended, hoping to secure a referral letter. Joe, the chief technology officer (CTO), was the complete opposite, knowledgeable, friendly, and approachable. He had moved from Virginia to chase his dream of founding a startup in Silicon Valley.

Patrick, who led sales, was your classic "sales guy." His days were filled with phone calls and doing pull-ups on a bar he'd installed over his office door. He frequented the local 24-hour fitness gym at all hours, seeming driven yet easily distracted. I often wondered how he managed to close deals when he was constantly working out or attending social events in the evenings.

We often ordered lunch together and headed up to the roof, sitting on whatever boxes we could find, soaking in the city views. Over time, it seemed the social life and distractions caught up with Patrick. Years later, while scrolling through LinkedIn, I learned that the trio had parted ways. Patrick had left the company to found his own medical startup, which was later acquired by a well-known tech firm. The startup where I interned continued to grow for several years before being acquired by another profitable company. All three founders have since continued their journeys in the tech world, each carving their own path.

Unfortunately, I experienced a minor hiccup during my internship in San Francisco that overcomplicated my plans for those two months.

During the second week of the internship, a group of interns decided to go out for some drinks. I was concerned, as I wasn't drinking at all in San Francisco and didn't want to start. I wasn't experiencing anxiety like I had back home, which seemed to be a good sign. I started to think that being in a different environment was actually making things better for me. All I wanted to do was work, study, learn, and reflect on my time there. I wanted to embrace and soak in every opportunity I could.

That same night, before even having a single drink, I tripped climbing the stairs of the bar and snapped the ligaments in my left ankle, the very same ankle I'd injured as a teenager. It felt like life was testing me yet again. My ankle immediately swelled up, and I couldn't walk or even move it. A drag queen outside, smoking a cigarette, noticed me struggling on the steps and kindly helped me inside. The bartender, seeing my pain, offered me a shot. "On the house! Take your pick," he said. I replied, "I guess I will do Jägermeister," that was my shot of choice in my early twenties, classy, I know. At that moment, I would have taken anything to distract me from the pain. I downed a cold shot of Jägermeister as someone called for a ride.

It was 2013, so Lyft wasn't around yet, and Uber was a luxury-only service, way pricier than a cab. Instead, the driver arrived in a car from Homobile, a service with a catchy, yet hilarious slogan: "Taking ho's where they need to go." It was designed to shuttle drag queens from club to club between shows. As I sat there, I couldn't help but laugh, thinking, Only I could find myself in a situation like this.

I still keep a manila envelope full of memories from that internship, and tucked inside is their business card. Thanks to that driver, I made it to the ER.

I was out of commission for the next few weeks, confined to my apartment while I recovered. Thankfully, I could work remotely, and the team was supportive. A few friends from work even stopped by with groceries and checked in regularly. During that stretch, I survived mostly on peanut butter and jelly sandwiches and takeout.

As I focused on healing, my mom suggested a wheelchair might help me get around the city. I asked my dad to help cover the cost, but he only managed to rent one for a few days before telling me he couldn't spare any more money. It was a tough moment, one that made me start questioning my decisions, but I was determined not to let it ruin the rest of my experience. So I tackled San Francisco's infamous hills on crutches.

One afternoon, everyone decided to visit Lombard Street, the "crookedest street in the world." I had missed enough sightseeing already and didn't want to sit this one out. So I joined, crutches and all. As we made our way down the winding path, a group of tourists spotted me carefully making my way and started clapping and cheering me on. We all laughed. It felt like a scene pulled straight from an '80s movie.

Later that same week, I hobbled into a local karaoke night, determined to have a little fun. At some point, tensions flared and people started arguing. In the chaos, no one noticed a crisp hundred-dollar bill on the floor. Balancing on my crutches, I managed to scoop it up and, without missing a beat, shouted, "Winner, winner, chicken dinner!" They all went silent, then everyone burst into laughter.

Overall, the internship was a life-changing opportunity that opened doors I never imagined would be available to me. It left a lasting impact on my life. For the first time, learning felt not just rewarding but truly meaningful. By the end of the internship, my plan to connect with Jeff had paid off. I made it a point to help him with a problem no one else could solve. His computer kept crashing and the error logs offered no clues. Although my backgroud was not in IT, I was determined to find a solution. After some trial and error, I finally identified the issue and resolved it.

When the last week of the internship came around, I knocked on Jeff's slightly closed door and asked him for a reference letter. He agreed without hesitation and had it done that same day. At the very least, this was a sign I was heading in the right direction. Months later, that letter helped me secure the job that launched my career in tech. When the internship wrapped up, we exchanged emails and social media contacts, promising to stay in touch. Many of the interns dreamed of returning to the city permanently, though none of us had concrete plans to make it happen.

The day to leave finally arrived, and as I packed my belongings, memories of my time in the city kept replaying in my mind. When the plane took off from California, heading back to Puerto Rico, a wave of anxiety washed over me. I feared that all the career progress I'd made would start to unravel the moment I landed. But within minutes, a new clarity emerged. I wanted to make San Francisco my permanent home. I didn't have a detailed plan yet, but I was determined to make it happen. Life felt different there. No one knew me, and for the first time, I could start fresh and become the person I'd always believed I was meant to be.

After coming home, I told my family I was moving back permanently and started selling off the few belongings I'd left behind. I don't think anyone truly believed me, but at that point, nothing was going to stop me. I sold my old Jeep for $2,000. Honestly, it was falling apart, so how I made any money off it is still beyond me. Finding a company in California willing to take a chance on me was a real struggle. I spent over months scouring job boards and applying online with no luck. Eventually, I decided to take a more direct approach and flew to San Francisco to attend meetups and talk to recruiters face-to-face. I had a few meetings lined up, hoping one of them might open a door.

At the time, my ex Lisa was working for an airline. We were still on decent terms, and she shared some "buddy passes" with me. Thanks to her, I was able to fly for under fifty bucks. We never rekindled the relationship or formed a deep friendship, but we stayed in touch, texting a few times a month

While I was there, I stayed in a budget hotel not far from where I'd lived during my internship.

Circa 2013

On my first evening there, I went to a networking event within walking distance of the hotel.

As I ordered a drink at the bar to help me mingle, the universe conspired in my favor. Sipping on an Anchor Steam beer, I happened to meet Clarence Johnson. This man is the definition of a social butterfly. He knew everyone in the room, and you would see people raise their glasses and smile as he made his way around. He had been living in San Francisco for years and worked as a designer in the tech industry. When he wasn't working, he was meeting the locals and growing his network. We ended up chatting for some time, and I told him I was looking to step into the tech industry in San Francisco and leave my life in Puerto Rico behind. He asked, "Why leave a vacation spot to come to the city?"

I smiled and replied, "I've outgrown the island, it's time for a new adventure."

He was a kind man who introduced me to several contacts at the meetup to help with my job search. Later that night, he gathered a few people, and we headed to another bar called Tunnel Top. It felt like the Cheers of San Francisco. Everyone knew each other by name. After some drinks, we all grabbed late-night snacks at Mel's Drive-In. That night, I met several startup founders. Now, years later, it's wild to see who actually made it and who had to close their doors. Silicon Valley either puts you in the right place at the right time, helping you build the connections you need to succeed, or it chews you up and spits you out.

As I was heading back to the hotel, we exchanged numbers, and over the next few years, Clarence became a true friend in San Francisco. We attended many more events together, building a genuine connection. Then, in 2016, I was shocked to see on social media that he had passed away from an aneurysm just before his forty-second birthday. The news hit me hard, not only because of his sudden loss but also because I wasn't there in San Francisco to say goodbye, to share one last drink. I was comforted to learn that several local spots paid tribute to him and Tunnel Top even put up a sign in his honor. Life is incredibly fragile, yet we often don't realize it until moments like this remind us how precious it truly is.

When I returned to Puerto Rico after a week of job hunting in San Francisco, I knew I was determined to do whatever it took to make the move happen. I had to keep pushing, even when my faith wavered. I chose not to renew my apartment lease and sold almost everything, keeping only my laptop, Xbox, and clothes. For a few months, I moved in with my father while I figured out my next steps.

Eleven years later, I came to understand just how much I should have cherished that time. I took on odd freelancing gigs to get by until I could make the move to San Francisco. Then one day, an email arrived that changed everything. It was a response to a technical recruiter role I'd applied for weeks earlier. I saw this as my chance to break into the tech startup world. My "master plan," or what I thought was one, was to accept the recruiter role and, while helping others land jobs, use those same skills to find my own position in tech. I figured being in San Francisco would make interviews easier, and the plan felt simple and straightforward.

I'd embellished my application a bit, listing the address of the apartment I stayed in during my internship. The very next day, I flew to San Francisco with whatever savings I had left and booked the cheapest hotel I could find. The final round of interviews was with the director, a lesbian woman, and we seemed to hit it off right away. I think she saw something of herself in me, and whether it was luck or kindness, I had a strong feeling she was going to offer me the job.

After several days of interviews, I flew back to Puerto Rico, weighed down by an intense existential crisis. I saw this as my one last chance to start fresh, a final shot to leave Puerto Rico behind and build a new life in San Francisco. Time and money were running out, and I was struggling to keep hope alive. Sleep eluded me for days. Then, just when I needed it most, I received the call that would change everything.

They offered me the technical recruiter job, but the pay was far from enough to live comfortably in the city. Still, it was now or never, so I accepted immediately. Within weeks, I sold the rest of my belongings and packed my bags. I moved with just three suitcases, my laptop, Xbox, a job offer, some savings, and no place to call home. Something inside me pushed me forward. I was transforming into a new version of myself, filled with hope for a better future. It felt like all the pieces were finally falling into place, and the universe was finally lending me a helping hand, rewarding all my hard work.

We had a small BBQ at my dad's house before I left. As I sat outside chatting with my mom, aunt, dad, Mario Jr., Viviana, and the kids, Viviana kept repeating, "You won't have enough money to make it in San Francisco. With rent, electricity, and water, you'll barely be able to afford food." I was furious. Why did she feel the need to say that, knowing I was leaving in just two days?

What I really wanted to say was, "Just wish me good luck, and tell me that if things don't work out, I can always come home." Looking back now as an adult, I can see the intentions were good, even if the delivery wasn't ideal. At the time, I was a 25-year-old completely overwhelmed, moving across the country with barely any money, a dream, and no place to call home. That night, I left feeling determined to prove everyone wrong. My life's purpose became showing my family I wouldn't fail, which, looking back, wasn't the healthiest motivation. Your purpose in life should be guided by what you believe in, not by the need to prove others wrong. I ended up learning that later in life. As I said goodbye to my family, I also had to say goodbye to my grandfather, who had always believed in me and even paid for my dorm during my internship. That was the hardest part. I was deeply saddened too. Despite it all, I knew this was the right step for me to move forward. I had never seen him cry before, but he did that day. Even in his sadness, I believe he understood that this was what I needed.

A New Chapter in California

My mother, understandably uneasy about the move, decided to come with me for two weeks to help me get settled. On the way to San Francisco, we stopped in Florida for a few days to visit extended family. We landed in the city on February 1, 2013, with no place to stay. So, I booked a room at the same no-frills hotel I had used during my interview trip. It's since closed down, but it was tucked away on the corner of Mission and Minna. The rooms were simple, bed frames made from reclaimed wood, a small table in the corner, and just enough to get by.

On the flight there, I grabbed the napkin from my seltzer water and began jotting down a list, a kind of blueprint for the life I hoped to build. This wasn't just a move; it felt like a clean slate. I wanted to meet new friends, find a serious relationship with someone from a different culture, so we could learn and grow together, land a job, find a place to live, chase happiness, and eventually, buy that luxury car I'd always dreamed of.. That car was the only material thing on my list. Everything else was about building a life that felt rich in meaning.

I opened my journal and pinned the napkin between two pages. Creating that list brought me back to my days as an intern, when I used to wander the city, jotting down observations and reflections in the margins of my notebook. One afternoon, while heading to a nearby pharmacy, I noticed an apartment building in a prime spot right on Market Street. On a whim, I scribbled down the address, thinking, *Just in case I ever need this.*

Now, as I flipped through that same journal on my flight back to San Francisco, the address caught my eye. That building became the first place I visited in my search for an apartment.

The apartment address was the only lead I had, a single shot at finding a place to live. It would either work out, or I'd be back to square one. When we arrived in San Francisco, my mom and I settled into the hotel. I scheduled a viewing for the apartment two days later, which felt like a tight window considering I had just six days to find housing before starting my new job the following week.

The next morning, mom and I decided to venture into the city. My mother had never been to San Francisco so naturally I wanted to show her around. But beneath the sightseeing plans was something deeper I wanted her to see that I could make it on my own. We spent the afternoon at Fisherman's Wharf, where the scent of sourdough bread and fresh seafood filled the air. While mom stepped away to use the restroom, I stood alone in the middle of the crowd, just soaking it all in, the energy, the noise, the feeling that anything could happen. That's when I felt a light tap on my right shoulder. I turned around to find a woman I'd never seen before. She looked directly at me and said, "You came here to find success and happiness, but you'll fall in love here." Then she turned and vanished into the crowd.

Who was that I thought? What did she mean? I laughed it off, thinking maybe she was just a quirky local. But she wasn't wrong. Exactly one month later, I met the woman who would become my wife. Years later, my mother told me that on her way to the bathroom that very same day, the same woman had stopped her as well. She looked at my mom and said, "Your daughter will find success here," before once again disappearing into the crowd. I still don't know who she was, but I've never forgotten that moment.

After a few days of exploring the city like tourists, the day of the apartment viewing finally arrived. I was both excited and anxious as we left our hotel and made our way to Market Street.

The moment we stepped into the lobby, I was struck by how grand it felt, high ceilings, polished black marble floors, and a fountain in the center where people could sit and gaze out through the glass doors. It felt more like a hotel than an apartment building. As we walked toward the leasing office, I noticed it was connected to a Starbucks and a bakery, which made me instantly think, this is probably way out of my budget.

We were shown the smallest available unit: a five hundred square foot apartment with a small balcony overlooking City Hall. Despite its size, it felt full of potential, a blank slate in the heart of the city. I sat down to fill out the application, crossed my fingers, and silently hoped for the best.

They told me they'd need to run my credit and call a few references before making a final decision, so all I could do was wait.

After what felt like an endless wait, I was finally approved and, to my surprise, the apartment was reasonably priced. I completed the official paperwork and paid the security deposit:

just two hundred dollars. It was so low, even by 2013 standards, that to this day, people in San Francisco are shocked when I tell them. That small number gave me a little more breathing room in my budget and meant I could stretch my savings further while figuring out side hustles to make ends meet.

The building was in a prime location for someone starting fresh in California. It had originally been a hotel, now converted into apartments. The layout still carried that hotel room feel, narrow hallway, compact living space, but somehow, it still felt like a home.

That night, lying on the bed back in the hotel, I felt relieved. I had found a place to live. I reached for my journal, flipped to the page where I had once scribbled the apartment's address, and added a new detail: #1512. I wrote the date beside it—February 15, 2013—the day I officially became a Californian.

The two weeks flew by, but not without their share of bumps. My mother suddenly fell ill and had to be hospitalized. Between the demands of my new job, a half-empty apartment, and figuring out how to travel back and forth from the hospital, I was overwhelmed. I had no idea what to do. She couldn't fly back home on her own, and I found myself spiraling, unsure of the next step. It didn't take long for my boss to mention over Thai food at lunch that I seemed disengaged at work.

Amid back-and-forth conversations with family about how we could possibly get help, our cousin Tina stepped in. She came to stay for a few days as Mom recovered. I'm not sure I've ever told her just how much that moment could have changed the path of my future in San Francisco. I could have lost my job and my new apartment in the blink of an eye. Words will never measure my gratitude. My mother and Tina flew back to Puerto Rico, and suddenly, I was alone in my new apartment, just me, four walls, and the quiet hum of a new beginning. My mom had left behind a handwritten note for me, which I found folded neatly on the dining table. In it, she wrote that she hoped this journey would lead me to whatever it was my heart was searching for.

Circa 2013

During those first two weeks in San Francisco, I managed to furnish the essentials: a bed, a dining table, a leatherette futon, a small three-drawer dresser, and a TV. I even found a tiny table for fifteen dollars that became my makeshift nightstand. It wasn't much, but it was enough to make the apartment feel like mine.

As I settled into my new apartment and shaped it into a cozy, livable space, I felt a surge of excitement for the adventures that awaited me.

In those first weeks, I woke up every morning at 5:30 a.m., stepping out onto my fifteenth-floor balcony to watch the San Francisco fog roll in. From that height, nestled in the heart of downtown, I could just make out the top of the Golden Gate Bridge in the distance, a view so surreal. Coming from an apartment with a dusty dirt-patch parking lot, seeing that iconic bridge from my window was a powerful reminder that I was exactly where I needed to be.

Biking The Golden Gate Bridge

Deep down, I knew the real work was just beginning, but I was ready to meet it head-on. Gradually, a routine formed: crossing the street, hopping on the F line streetcar to Montgomery, where my office was. I quickly became a familiar face at the coffee shop on the building's first floor, and before long, my Americano with a splash of cream was waiting for me, reliably ready at 7:30 sharp.

The owner, a friendly older Latino man who always wore a polo shirt and khakis, quickly noticed my daily visits and made it a point to greet me each time. One quiet morning, we finally had the chance to chat. He shared that he had come to the city with barely any money, working his way through several restaurant jobs before saving enough to open this tiny coffee shop in the financial district. The shop was no bigger than a hallway, barely room for customers to stand while ordering. Yet, every morning, he greeted everyone from hipsters to suited professionals with a warm smile. This coffee shop was his dream, and you could tell he was savoring every moment of it. I was captivated by the stories of people throughout the city, their journeys, how they arrived, and the hard work they poured into chasing their dreams. Their experiences sparked the inspiration I needed to keep going.

On the other hand, I found myself struggling with my technical recruiter job. I just wasn't a natural salesman. Still, I was determined to make it a stepping stone toward the future I wanted to build.

My first week on the job turned out to be more than just an exciting new opportunity—it was an eye-opener. I quickly learned that racism in America isn't always loud or obvious; it's often woven into everyday interactions.

Growing up in Puerto Rico, I never felt different because of my skin color or my name. Everyone around me had Spanish last names, and with my light skin, I was considered white. While racism does exist on the island, especially toward darker-skinned Puerto Ricans, I personally hadn't experienced it. Neither had many of my friends, at least not in a way that was openly discussed.

To most people here, nothing about my appearance says "Puerto Rican." I could walk down any street and pass as white, unassuming. That changed when the CEO of the recruiting firm where I'd just started learned my name, Marita Espada, and found out I was from Puerto Rico.

One Monday morning during our stand-up meeting, he suddenly said, "I love Mexico City, Marita." I replied, "That's great. I've never been."

He looked confused. "Aren't you from there? What's your favorite food? I love quesadillas."

I had to correct him: "No, I'm Puerto Rican."

Switching to Spanish, he continued: "Oye, ¿cómo estás?"

I answered, "Bien," but in my head I was thinking, "Bien, pendejo."

He kept going, tossing out random Spanish phrases like he was showing off. That's when a coworker named Lauren, who sat behind me, finally cut in and said, "She's from Puerto Rico, not Mexico City. Yes, they both speak Spanish, but Puerto Rico is an island, not a country like Mexico. Very different cultures."

I turned around and quietly said, "Thank you." One person, one brave person, stepped in to stop him from continuing his ignorant assumptions. He seemed unfazed by the correction, eventually stopping only because we had to refocus on our weekly call prep.

By the end of the day, I realized this was probably just the tip of the iceberg when it comes to the subtle and not-so-subtle racism in the U.S. The CEO, Michael, was a white man from Rochester, NY, with blond hair and blue eyes. His behavior didn't come from a place of curiosity or respect, just lazy stereotypes and unchecked bias. That same day, I also found out I now belong to another group I had never really thought about before: the Hispanic/Latino checkbox. That wasn't a thing growing up in Puerto Rico. How could it be? We were all just Puerto Rican.

Well. Level unlocked: Minority Checkbox #4.

As my first month in San Francisco drew to a close, feelings of loneliness and homesickness began to settle in. It wasn't that I wanted to return to Puerto Rico. I simply missed the comfort of familiarity, the feeling of being home and surrounded by people I knew.

Over time, I made a few friends at work, but we rarely saw each other outside the office. Most weekends, I was on my own, lost in my thoughts and planning various solo adventures. I'd explore the city, enjoy dinners alone, stroll through Dolores Park, and browse local shops. To earn extra money, I took on a side hustle dog-sitting some weekends. Despite the occasional loneliness that sometimes felt overwhelming, those days were some of the best of my life. That chapter shaped me into who I am today, and the solitude helped me grow in ways I never expected.

Finding My Heart In San Francisco

It was a Friday in March when my manager invited me to join her and another coworker for dinner. She was originally from New York, and one of her childhood friends, Karla, was visiting San Francisco with a friend. I agreed at first, but as the day wore on, I felt a growing urge to just head home after work. The weight of being completely alone in the city was beginning to sink in. I felt overwhelmed, and the homesickness that had been quietly lingering started to feel heavier than usual.

My coworker was persistent about me joining the dinner that Friday night. He called and texted multiple times, and eventually,

I gave in. I freshened up and walked to the nearest bus stop, stepped on, and was dropped off two blocks from the restaurant. When I arrived at Cha Cha Cha on Mission Street, the vibrant Latin music, colorful décor, and the aroma of the food immediately made me feel at home.

As I sat down, the table was already buzzing with conversation. Some people were eating and passing around tapas, and before I knew it, I was laughing and sharing stories about Puerto Rico. From across the table, as I shared a story I overheard a woman say, "My company has an office in Manatí, Puerto Rico." She was deep in conversation on her side of the table. She had long, flowing brown hair, big beautiful eyes, and a smile that was hard to ignore.

After dinner, as everyone began gathering their things and making their way to the restroom, I finally caught her name, Isabela. We quietly slipped away to the bar next door, thinking the others would join us shortly.

As we talked, I found myself increasingly curious about her, drawn in by the way she spoke and the ease of our conversation. Time slipped away from us, and it wasn't until much later that we realized no one from our group had come to join us at the bar. We made our way back to Cha Cha Cha to reconnect, then headed with everyone to a karaoke spot near Castro Street.

While others debated song choices and ordered another round of drinks, I finally worked up the nerve to ask Isabela for her number. My angle? Offering her a tour of San Francisco before she flew back to New Jersey. I figured, who could say no to a local's tour, even if that "local" had only been in the city for a month? I mean, I'd barely learned where the grocery store was, but I was ready to be a tour guide!

As much as I was looking forward to giving her that tour, we never got the chance to meet up again before she left the city. *Oh well,* I thought, if I ever find myself in New York, at least I'll know someone there. I genuinely liked her, there was real chemistry between us, but I didn't expect we'd ever cross paths again.

That Monday at work, my coworkers didn't hesitate to point out how well Isabela and I seemed to hit it off. I just laughed and said, "Even if we did, I'd never leave the city and move to New Jersey."

Unless, of course, I wanted to perfect my GTL routine, Gym, Tan, Laundry, like they do on MTV's Jersey Shore. Then maybe I'd consider it.

As the weeks passed, I slipped back into my routine, working, trying to make new friends, taking solo trips around the city on Saturdays, dog sitting, and spending Sundays reading and learning more about the tech industry. I was slowly settling into a typical American rhythm and beginning to find my footing.

Then, out of the blue, I got a text from Isabela: Hey, how are you? We hadn't spoken since that Friday night at Cha Cha Cha. What started as a single message soon turned into a steady stream. Texts became daily calls, and those calls evolved into weekend Skype dates over the course of several months.

We weren't exclusive, not officially, so I continued dating around in San Francisco. Still, no date ever compared to that one night with Isabela. Gradually, my interest in dating other women faded as we began planning trips to visit each other. What began as a casual connection was clearly becoming something more serious.

A few months later, while Isabela was still often on my mind, my thoughts began shifting toward a growing concern: my mother's health. She was scheduled for surgery, not life-threatening, but serious enough to worry me and the rest of the family. The procedure would be lengthy, and her recovery even more so. She had struggled for years with diverticulosis, and this operation was meant to finally bring her some relief. The plan was to remove about two feet of her intestine, the section causing the most trouble. It was an invasive surgery, one that involved cutting the affected portion and stapling the remaining ends together.

On one hand, I was deeply worried about my mom's health. On the other, I couldn't ignore the anxiety I felt about my own life and future. I had just been let go from my job as a technical recruiter, and the only thing that offered even a flicker of hope was my daily call with Isabela.

I was juggling a whirlwind of emotions, grief, fear, uncertainty, while trying to quiet the relentless voice of my inner critic. I felt like I was failing at everything. Moving from Puerto Rico had started to feel like a huge mistake, and I couldn't shake the fear that I'd made the wrong choice. The thought of my family finding out made it worse. Great, I thought. One more reason for them to believe I can't make it.

As if everything else wasn't enough, just two days before my mother's surgery, my grandfather was rushed to the hospital. My aunt later told me she knew he was gone the moment the EMTs opened the ambulance door. His arm had slipped lifelessly from the stretcher as they tried to resuscitate him.

My mom called to break the news. We didn't talk long. I didn't have much to say. I was just trying to hold it together. After I hung up, I sat in silence, feeling hollow at first, then overwhelmed by a wave of sadness. More than anything, I felt guilty for leaving, for not being there when he passed. He'd been so upset when I moved away. But I held onto one small comfort: I had visited Puerto Rico shortly before he died, and I got to see him one last time.

Not only had I lost my job, but my mother's surgery was looming in less than forty-eight hours and now my grandfather had passed away. It was too much to bear all at once. Without hesitation, I booked a flight to Puerto Rico for the very next day. I needed to be home. I needed to see my family. Though I was battling bronchitis and struggling to breathe, I somehow found the strength to keep moving forward.

As we neared the island, I could already hear the applause of fellow passengers. Puerto Rican tradition holds that clapping when the plane lands is a way to express relief, gratitude, and joy for a safe arrival. It's a heartfelt cultural ritual, a collective "thank you" to the pilots and crew.

When we touched down, everything felt different, like a piece of my heart had been left behind. At my grandfather's house, I sat at his desk and felt his presence all around me. He used to tell anyone who would listen that his granddaughter was working in San Francisco, doctors, the front desk staff, strangers. His pride was unmistakable.

As I sat there grieving in silence, I knew I had to gather myself to visit my mother, who had decided to go ahead with her surgery. Thankfully, it went well, and she was able to come home shortly after.

I stayed in Puerto Rico a little longer, keeping busy as if I had work to do, while quietly looking for a new job. Those old feelings of doubt slowly crept back, but I wasn't quite ready to share that I was unemployed with anyone.

When I left Puerto Rico, I had a connecting flight in Florida where I met up with Isabela. She was interviewing for a job there, so we finally had our first official date. I stayed with her in Miami for a few days, and we shared dinner at Havana 1957 on Española Way. It was such a memorable night. I couldn't remember the last time I'd felt that excited about a first date. She made me laugh, made me feel alive, and for those hours, it felt like the world just faded away, leaving only the two of us.

As the months went by, we settled into a rhythm, flying back and forth across the country on alternating months—one month I visited her, the next she came to see me. It didn't take long for me to realize how deeply I saw my future with her. There was something in her deep, brown-caramel eyes that made me feel like I'd finally found home.

Once I returned to San Francisco, I dove headfirst into interviewing. I needed to land another tech job that would keep me in the city. To stretch my budget, I ate the same simple, low-cost meals every day, carefully saving every penny. My grocery list was straightforward: coffee, cereal, milk, rice, beans, Spam, bread, ham, and cheese. Nothing more, nothing less. It wasn't the healthiest diet, but it got me through: cereal for breakfast, Spam with rice and beans for lunch, and a sandwich for dinner. The only occasional luxury was buying coffee at a local café, just to leave the apartment for a few hours.

I was determined not to leave San Francisco feeling like a failure, even though that shadow of doubt lingered constantly. I kept all of this to myself. I didn't want my family to know. I knew they'd help if I asked, but I also feared they'd later use my struggles as proof that I couldn't make it on my own, that without their support, I was doomed to fail again.

After going through several interview rounds and facing many rejections, including a contract position interview at Google, I finally received the offer I had been hoping for.

I landed an implementation lead role at a small startup called YouNoodle, a company that developed a platform used by governments, universities, corporations, and foundations to organize and manage entrepreneurship competitions. In this role, I had the chance to support and empower people with dreams of launching their own startups, helping ambitious founders turn those dreams into reality.

The team was small, just fifteen people total across product, engineering, marketing, and more. Our office was tucked away in the basement of a brick-walled building, complete with a game room that had a ping-pong table and shuffleboard. I was making $20,000 more than in my previous technical recruiting role, and the offer included a stock package. Plus, we had deals with two local restaurants, so all fifteen of us enjoyed free breakfast and lunch every day.

Meanwhile, my dog walking and sitting side hustle was gaining traction—I had a solid client list, and some pups even stayed with me regularly. Between both gigs, I was finally earning enough to live a modestly comfortable life in San Francisco.

My daily routine involved taking the Muni from Van Ness to the 4th and King Street station, passing by the stadium of my favorite team, the San Francisco Giants. Then I'd walk two blocks to The Creamery, just across from Caltrain, where I'd grab a large black coffee and a breakfast sandwich. From there, I'd cross the street and head into the office. Settling at my desk with breakfast in hand, I'd dive into emails, plan my day, prep notes for meetings, check in with engineering about bugs and issues, and finish the afternoon sharpening my ping-pong skills with colleagues.

My tech career had officially begun, and I was thrilled by all the possibilities ahead. I started building meaningful relationships with people who recognized the value I could bring, and my friends began inviting me out on weekends. I found myself working late into the night at my apartment, and whenever someone at the office needed help with a project, I was always the first to volunteer. Sometimes I didn't fully know what I was doing, but I took on projects that gave me enough time to learn the skills I needed along the way. I wasn't about to miss a single opportunity; I grabbed every one that came my way.

Circa 2013

Over time, I had the chance to work with many seasoned leaders and tech experts throughout Silicon Valley. Through my job and connections, I found opportunities to collaborate and present at Google, Salesforce, and even Ivy League universities.

I led boot camps for interns from Mexico who wanted to experience Silicon Valley's work culture and explore new opportunities. I partnered with companies like Intel and HP to run startup competitions, including Desafío Intel, which supported young innovators in South America by inspiring and empowering them on their entrepreneurial journeys. My role often involved acting as a bridge for aspiring entrepreneurs, helping them leverage our company's resources to raise funding and scale their startups. We regularly organized sessions to refine elevator pitches and pitch decks.

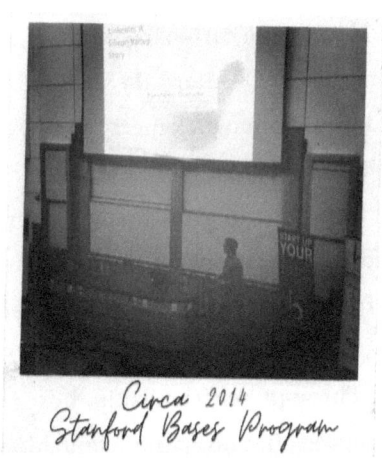

Circa 2014
Stanford Bases Program

One afternoon, while walking to a presentation at Stanford with a colleague, we were stopped by a man wearing a Blackberry shirt. After we moved on, I asked my colleague, "Who was that?" He just chuckled and said, "That was Steve Jobs's son."

I found myself in rooms with people I never imagined I'd have the chance to work alongside. I wasn't part of the Ivy League elite, yet there I was, sharing ideas and collaborating with them. At times, imposter syndrome crept in. I'd be sitting in expensive restaurants across the city, ordering dishes like tuna tartare and foie gras without even knowing what they were, only realizing once they arrived at the table and pretending to like them.

As my experience in tech grew, so did my network, which proved invaluable as I worked to build a successful career. I had a friend who was part of Uber in its early days when it was all about luxury black cars, and thanks to him, I enjoyed friends-and-family discounts. Naturally, I used those free rides to impress Isabela whenever she visited, taking her out to dinner around the city.

Another friend joined an early-stage startup as employee number ten, just before their IPO. After they went public, he bought an Aston Martin and would often pick me up for drives out to Walnut Creek, where we'd enjoy Cuban food. On those rides, we covered it all, everything from startup growth and funding rounds to the risks involved and my aspirations for my tech career.

I also had a friend named Christina, who left YouNoodle to launch her own startup, dedicating countless weekends to bring her vision to life. Through her friendship, I experienced genuine kindness and compassion, and gained valuable lessons in marketing, public speaking, and refining my writing skills.

As I continued networking my way through San Francisco, I attended a meetup where several C-level executives and mid-level managers shared their career journeys and how they had climbed into leadership roles. One woman stood out. When she took the stage, she spoke candidly about the toll her high-pressure job was taking on her personal life. Her role involved making decisions that affected not just her company, but thousands of people, and the stress was becoming overwhelming.

In her search for balance, she said she turned to meditation. She started small, using an app for just ten to fifteen minutes a day, and eventually began attending full retreats. At the time, I didn't think much of it, but her story stuck with me. Years later, I would come to understand why.

I began carving out small pockets of time during the day to meditate, though I didn't notice any real benefits at first. It wasn't until years later that it started to make sense. I came to understand that you don't find meditation—meditation finds you.

It wasn't until I stepped into a leadership role, facing the same stress and pressure I once heard others speak about, that my practice truly took root. That's when meditation became more than a curiosity. It became a tool. A way to ground myself, stay present, and create a greater sense of balance in my life.

As I poured long hours into my new role at the tech startup and continued to grow professionally, my relationship with Isabela was also deepening. Our once-a-month visits were no longer enough, and each goodbye at the airport became more painful than the last. The drives there often passed in silence, a blur of emotion, and every farewell left my heart a little heavier. It's true what they say: "Airports have seen more sincere kisses than wedding halls."

On one of our many visits, I traveled 2,560 miles to New Jersey and checked into a DoubleTree. Since Isabela was still living with her family, we usually stayed in hotels during my trips. I arrived first, giving me time to settle into the room and unpack. When she finally got there, I headed down to the lobby to meet her. As the elevator doors opened and I saw her, something shifted—I realized I was falling deeply in love with her. We'd been together for about six months, and lately, I'd catch myself daydreaming about a future together.

It became even more clear to me just how genuine our connection was right from the start, and here's why. We all have those shows, movies, or songs we turn to for comfort, whether we're sick, heartbroken, or just too drained to follow a new plot or set of characters. For me, that comfort show is *Friends*. I've watched it so many times I can quote entire scenes without missing a beat, often dropping lines into everyday conversations without even thinking. Thankfully, most of my friends and acquaintances are fans too, so they usually catch the references.

In the first season of *Friends*, there's a memorable episode where Ross is trying to come to terms with his divorce from Carol. He's in his new apartment with Joey and Chandler, assembling furniture and processing the end of a four-year marriage. As Ross reflects on the breakup, Joey and Chandler try to lift his spirits, encouraging him to move on. They tell him it's time to close that chapter—that there's someone else out there for him. Joey puts it in classic *Friends* fashion, comparing dating to ice cream: there are tons of flavors, and all Ross has to do is grab a spoon.

The following night, Ross is at Monica's and Rachel's apartment. After Monica heads to bed, Ross finds a quiet moment to confess to Rachel that he had a crush on her back in high school. With a knowing smile, she simply replies, "I know." Encouraged, Ross gently asks if he can take her out sometime. She doesn't say no. As Rachel heads off to bed, Ross grabs his coat, a quiet smile spreading across his face as he walks toward the door. On his way out, Monica on her way to the kitchen spots him and asks why he looks so happy. Ross replies, "I just grabbed a spoon," signaling that he's ready to move forward and open himself up to love again.

I was hesitant to fully commit, searching for reasons why things might not work—to shield myself from the inevitable heartbreak. I didn't feel about Isabela the same way I had about Lisa. I was, slowly but surely, falling deeply in love with her, a kind of love that I had never experienced before—the kind of love that one can only hope to have once in a lifetime. When I arrived back in San Francisco, I texted my friend Georgia. She was an avid fan of *Friends* as well, so she knew exactly what I meant when I texted her, "I grabbed a spoon."

Everything I had hoped for was starting to take shape, even though the road ahead remained long. I was working hard, building a career, nurturing a relationship, and finding ways to care for my mental health. I even tried to establish a gym routine, "tried" being the key word here. My early twenties, especially my time in San Francisco, constantly tested my values. I wasn't sure what truly mattered to me or what I was willing to stand firm on. Instead of simply following what others expected, I began deciding what my values should be. Over the following months and years, I filled my journal with worksheets, gradually defining those values. They became my compass, helping me find my truth, my voice, and guiding my decisions for years to come.

I was beginning to make choices that truly aligned with what was best for me, guided by my newly defined values like a North Star—free from the clouding effects of alcohol and adrenaline-fueled escapades. For the first time, my decisions were more deliberate and thoughtful. I was ready to make a change and build the life I had been envisioning.

I had been in my new job for nearly a year, and thoughts of a future with Isabela started to take shape. I was incredibly grateful for San Francisco and the people I'd met there, so the idea of leaving felt almost impossible. But with rent skyrocketing and friends moving out to the suburbs, I began to bring up the possibility of moving to New Jersey. Isabela was hesitant—her family didn't even know about us yet, and I could tell she wasn't ready to have that conversation. I knew she was scared, and honestly, beneath my excitement about us, I was scared too. Still, something inside urged me to trust my instincts, and this time, I felt certain I was right. Our relationship was far from typical—we started as friends, building a strong foundation before anything else. And all this time, we'd been long-distance, never living in the same state, much less the same town.

Even though I was making more calculated decisions overall, I didn't spend more than a month weighing this one. One Friday afternoon at happy hour, as we shared chips and salsa, I dropped the news about my move. My friend Jordy looked at me and asked, "How do you know this is the right move? Why not stay longer in California?" Without hesitation, I told him, "This is it, Jordy. I just know. Plus, the startup scene in NYC is booming—more and more startups are moving to the East Coast." No matter what anyone said, deep down I knew I was moving for my future wife.

I scoured Airbnb listings, checked out budget hotels nearby, and pared down my belongings as much as I could. The whole process moved quickly, but I felt confident I was choosing the right path forward. This wasn't my first big move, so I was no stranger to letting go of material things. As March 2014 came to a close, it was time to say goodbye to San Francisco after thirteen unforgettable months. I left my keys at the front desk, and a friend drove me to the airport. I still remember that drive vividly—passing by all the local spots where I'd made so many memories. I thought it was the last goodbye, even though it wasn't.

When I landed in New Jersey, doubt hit me hard. What if I'd made a mistake? What if Jordy was right? As I stepped out of the airport, my heart raced, my hands trembled, barely able to hold my suitcases. I knew that once I left those doors, there was no turning back. From my past, I'd learned not to put all my hopes and dreams on someone else. This move was my decision, to see if our relationship could grow while I pursued my tech career in NYC with my previous experience of working in Silicon Valley. I was still my own person, with my own goals and passions. Being a couple meant sharing life and dreams without losing who you are. That's where real growth begins.

After settling into a new chapter in New Jersey, I moved into a small apartment that Isabela owned as an investment property.

Her tenant had recently moved out, so the timing worked perfectly for me. Isabela was still living with her family, and we wanted to experience what a real relationship felt like, living separately but in the same state.

We had been together for just over a year, and our bond and love were growing stronger every day. I knew she loved me, I could see it in her actions, but she still kept a wall up, guarding herself after being deeply hurt in a past relationship. About a month earlier, I had told her I loved her, but she wasn't ready to say it back yet. I was disappointed, but I didn't push her. I was willing to be patient.

One summer, I flew from Newark to San Juan to visit family for a few days. After a week filled with delicious food, quality time with loved ones, and a few dinners with friends, it was time to head back. This time, I was flying from San Juan to JFK. As I settled into my seat, I texted my family and Isabela to let them know the plane was about to take off.

The plane slowly began taxiing, gradually picking up speed from twenty miles per hour to thirty, then forty—when suddenly, a loud explosion shook the aircraft. The engine had caught fire. I looked out the window just as panic erupted around me. Passengers screamed, grabbed backpacks, and scrambled for exits as the pilot slammed on the brakes, bringing the plane to an emergency stop.

In an instant, the flight attendants sprang into action, opening the emergency doors and deploying the inflatable slides. It was nighttime, and the cabin was pitch black—except for the eerie glow of the emergency aisle strips lighting the way.

Circa 2014

Thanks to JetBlue for helping me check off a bucket list item I never asked for, sliding down a plane's emergency slide. Honestly, I was just hoping for a good nap, maybe a drink, and some free chips.

I grabbed my phone and wallet from the seat pocket and hurried toward the slide. Just as I was about to go down, I noticed a young boy crying nearby. I reached for his hand and scanned the cabin for his parents. His father was helping an older couple stuck between seats, clearly panicked. I called out, "I'll take him and wait for you outside!" He waved back, squeezed through the seats, and shouted, "Okay!"

We slid down together onto the runway and made our way to the grass. Shortly after, the boy's father caught up to us. "Thank you for taking him," he said, and I replied, "No problem." As they walked away, I called Isabela. My shock quickly turned into panic, my voice trembling as I explained what had happened. She was distraught on the other end. After hanging up, my hands shook so much I struggled to put my phone away.

Two days later, Some how I mustered the courage to board another plane. Before takeoff, I texted my family and Isabela that we were about to depart.

In the last minutes right before takeoff, I received a text message from Isabela with just three words.

"I love you."

Despite her fear, she spoke the truth I'd known all along. And in that moment, my heart was full.

Riley Joins the Story

After countless conversations, Isabela and I finally made it official; we were moving in together. We toured several rental listings before settling on a cozy two-bedroom, two-bath apartment with a small outdoor deck. It felt like the perfect space to begin this new chapter side by side.

To lock it in, we needed to drop off a security deposit, so we headed to the bank. As we pulled up, my eyes drifted toward the pet shop next door. I'd been quietly wanting a dog for a while, especially after spending so much time dog-sitting back in San Francisco.

Curiosity got the best of us, and we wandered inside. Near the front, a woman was cradling a tiny cockapoo, cooing over it as she explained, "She's beautiful, but my husband won't let me have any more dogs."

The puppy was truly adorable: tiny, with a soft caramel coat, curly hair, and a little sweater that had a hole in it. Still, I didn't think adopting her was actually in the cards. We continued petting the other dogs, but as the cockapoo returned to her kennel, she gave me this look, eyes full of quiet hope. I asked to hold her, and the moment she was in my arms, I knew: she was coming home with us.

After going through the references and paperwork, everything was approved, and we brought her home. We debated names for a bit. She was "Frankie" for a whole hour before landing on Riley. It just fit. These days, she goes by Riled Up Riley if you follow her adventures on Instagram.

Riley quickly became the center of our world. She brought so much joy, and in many ways, helped us grow even closer. With her, it started to feel like we were becoming the kind of family I had always dreamed of.

After nearly three years together, navigating a cross-country move, job changes, and adopting a puppy, the moment finally arrived. In November of 2016, after nearly a year of quietly saving and planning, I found the courage to propose to Isabela. I chose a beautiful park where we'd once spent an afternoon with her niece. Something about that visit had stayed with me. It was peaceful, simple, and full of quiet joy. Just the three of us, and yet it felt like everything I needed.

I had made a mental note of that place the day we visited. I knew it had to be the spot. When the time came, surrounded by her family, I asked her to marry me in that same park. That memory, standing there with her, in a place that had made New Jersey feel like home, still stays with me. I'm not sure if it was the stillness of the moment or the feeling of certainty, but even now, that park feels like the place where everything aligned.

Still, we didn't get married for another two years. Isabela wasn't keen on having a wedding, while I felt strongly that we should do something to mark the occasion. We went back and forth more times than I can remember.

"Isabela, I really think we should do something small, maybe near a beach? Puerto Rico?" I suggested. She shook her head. "No, that would mean too many people having to travel." And so the conversation continued, for months.

For me, it wasn't just about planning a wedding. It was about honoring everything we had built together. I believed we deserved that day. That we had earned the right to celebrate our love, especially in front of the people who hadn't always believed in us. For many, we redefined what a family could look like, what it could be. And I was proud of that. Proud of who I had become, and proud of what Isabela and I had built together.

We got married by the Hudson River on a bright but chilly Friday in April 2018, with the New York City skyline as our backdrop. I remember trying to hold back tears as Isabela walked down the aisle to Ben Folds's *The Luckiest*.

April 2018

And I truly did feel like the luckiest that day. Growing up, I often wondered if I would ever find real love, if someone would see me, choose me, stay. I couldn't believe someone as brilliant and beautiful as Isabela had picked me.

As we built a life together, that old failure mindset I carried for so long started to fade. Every time I doubted myself, Isabela reminded me of who I really was. Through the years, she has become a beautiful reminder that sometimes not all we feel or think about ourselves is true. We've now been together for eleven years.

And no, not every chapter has been perfect. We've had our share of highs and lows. But when I look back at old photos, at smiling faces frozen in time, I've come to realize that the real story lives in the moments between the pictures. That's where life truly happens.

As I write this, I'm sitting at my desk in our townhome, waiting for our new house to be built, a single-family home, our first. After our wedding in 2018, we bought a two-bedroom townhouse with a loft. At the time, we weren't sure whether we wanted a newborn or if parenthood was even something we wanted to embark on. I leaned more toward the idea of having a child, but Isabela didn't feel as strongly about raising children. We were both fully immersed in demanding careers, and my job had me traveling constantly.

After a lot of conversations and soul-searching, we decided to attend an info session on fostering. It felt like the right step, a way to make a meaningful impact without having all the answers up front. Eventually, after navigating endless paperwork, background checks, and hours of training, we were certified.

We officially became foster parents, a path that's as rewarding as it is challenging, and absolutely not for the faint of heart. To date, we've had the privilege of fostering many children... and counting. Ultimately, we found a middle ground and chose this path to parenthood, a path that can be just as demanding, and at times even more so, than raising biological children. As a foster parent, you often become just a chapter, a page, or sometimes only a paragraph in a child's story. Your role is temporary, but your impact can be lasting. You show up, do your best, and try to be a steady, positive presence during whatever time you're given.

Sometimes, I still wonder if I'll miss out or one day regret not experiencing the full arc of parenthood, especially the early days with a newborn. It's a difficult thought to sit with, let alone say out loud. For a long time, I felt alone in this uncertainty, as if everyone else knew exactly what they'd do if faced with the same choice. But the more honest conversations I had with friends, the more I realized I wasn't alone. This is a complex, deeply personal decision, and neither path is easy. Both come with trade-offs, pros and cons, and no perfect answers.

There's no universal roadmap every relationship is different, and what's right for one couple might not be right for another.

As I write this book, I'm still evolving, still peeling back the layers that life keeps revealing. Remember that list I scribbled on a napkin during my flight to San Francisco? I've checked off every single item. I made friends from all over the world and immersed myself in different cultures. I didn't just find a girlfriend; I married a woman whose background is different from mine, she is beautiful and exceptionally smart. Isabela's intelligence and kindness inspire me every day. I didn't just land a job; I built a career and eventually carved out a passion around writing and podcasting.

In my mid-twenties, standing on what felt like the edge of a cliff, I came to a realization: life isn't something to wait for, it's something to create. It's about designing my own path amid the noise and chaos of the world. Yet, even after all that clarity, one question still stayed with me: what does "more" truly mean for me?

I wanted to define happiness on my own terms. I began sketching it out on paper, breaking it down piece by piece, unpacking each element in detail. I consciously chose to manifest my vision, working tirelessly on a master plan and carefully mapping out the steps to reach my goals. As I grew into the person I aspired to be, I discovered tools that supported my journey. In the chapters ahead, I'll share these tools with you.

A few months ago, while meditating, a vivid image came to me: my younger self bodysurfing, patiently waiting for the perfect wave. Back then, I didn't realize it, but that stillness, being gently rocked by the ocean, was my favorite part of the sport. It was the rare moment when I felt truly patient, fully focused, and completely present with just the sea and myself. It was the only time I wasn't overwhelmed by the fear of being alone with my own thoughts. As I've grown and transformed my life, I continue striving to become a better version of myself—for me and for those around me. I'm learning to offer myself grace, to embrace fresh starts, and to forgive myself when I stumble.

I realized that the responsibility was always mine—no one was coming to rescue me. It was up to me to find the tools and the strength to shape my life into what I truly wanted. For a long time, I blamed my circumstances—where I was born, the people around me, and everything else—but eventually, I had to stop pointing fingers and start making my own choices. The truth was, the path I needed wasn't out there in success, money, or material things. It wasn't about ticking off society's checklist. Instead, it was about looking inward, discovering what aligned with my values and goals. Now, when I see photos of my younger self, I wish I could say: "Relax. Don't worry so much. Trust that no matter what, you'll be okay."

There's a quote by Pema Chödrön that captures this perfectly: "You are the sky; everything else is the weather." Amid all the storms and turbulence in my life, there I was, just myself, steady and present. My first step was gaining a clear understanding of my values to set a meaningful direction for my life. Our values are the fundamental beliefs that form the foundation of who we are, they are like the foundation of a home. They guide and inspire us, helping us decide what actions to take and shaping the kind of person we strive to be, as well as how we treat ourselves and others. For a long time, I was wandering without clarity or awareness of my values. Discovering them became central to my life, because knowing yourself is essential to understanding your mind and behavior. If you want to explore this for yourself, I've included the template I use in this book. I review it regularly, at least once every New Year's Eve, because our values evolve as we grow and move into new chapters of this incredible journey called life.

Using this worksheet, I began by identifying my core values, things like family and community, and then I outlined the principles that give those values their shape, such as integrity, creativity, freedom, or inner peace. Next, I focused on my aesthetic values, the simple pleasures that bring me comfort and grounding, like savoring a cup of coffee, writing, or taking a walk while listening to an audiobook. Finally, I explored my counterfeit values, the beliefs and ideals I had inherited or been taught to accept as my own but didn't truly resonate with me.

Recognizing these was crucial because understanding who we are not only helps clarify who we truly are, it reveals what comes next, and uncovers how our renegade beliefs have formed.

You can find a free copy of my values worksheet
by visiting https://maritaespada.com
or scan the QR code below:

2

A RENEGADE'S JOURNEY

The unexamined life is not worth living.
—Socrates

O n a foggy, rainy night in San Francisco in February 2013, I came across the quote above for the very first time. Once I read it, I realized that my drive to find meaning and purpose still stirs a restless energy within me today. This restlessness keeps my focus locked on the future, often leaving little room to pause, reflect and focus on the present moment.

As a result, this sparked many quiet, solitary nights in my apartment. While others were out late in the bars and clubs of the Castro, I devoted hours to reading, researching, and learning. In a way, I was trying to draw wisdom from others instead of starting with a blank slate, hoping that within the pages of memoirs and articles, I might find answers to this constant restless feeling. Of course, part of the restlessness stemmed from my ADHD but at the time, it felt like something deeper was stirring beneath the surface.

Unpacking Performance

In part due to this restless feeling that many of us experience, we hardly ever take a moment to reflect on our lifestyles, relationships, or daily routines unless something happens that forces us to stop and think. More specifically, we rarely think about how we make decisions and how that can impact us, impact our ability to take action, get things done, reach goals, or plan for the life we want. Most of the time, we fall into habits that keep us going but can also put us on autopilot if we're not careful. Since 2013, I've made it a habit to pause and review my life every year.

Through this process, I've gone through different versions of myself, growing by learning new things and gaining clearer insights into how I view the world. From time to time, I look back at those earlier versions to see how much I've changed, what triggered those shifts, and whether they've helped me become the person I want to be.

During my first three months in San Francisco, I discovered audiobooks and quickly fell down a rabbit hole. I devoured books during my commute to work, while running errands, and even when meeting up with friends. There was always a personal growth audiobook playing in the background. It probably became an unhealthy obsession, but that's when performance within my world became something I needed to learn more about. I started with all the free content, free chapters of books, making notes if I thought they were worth listening to or even worth the $15 I would have to shell out to listen to the whole thing. If being cheap or frugal were a middle name, I'd have it on my birth certificate.

It all lead me to think that stepping back and seeing our lives from a wider perspective helps us spot areas where we can focus to build a richer, more meaningful life. But putting those insights into action? That's usually the toughest step.

I quickly learned that performance and decision-making are closely linked because the quality of your decisions often directly impacts how well you perform in any task, goal or overall in your life.

In a nutshell this is how they tie in together:

Good Decision-Making Fuels High Performance

1. **Effectiveness:** Well-informed, timely decisions lead to better outcomes, directly enhancing overall performance.
2. **Efficiency:** Strong decision-making helps you allocate your resources—like time, energy, and money—more wisely.

Performance Relies on Decision Quality

1. **Risk Management:** Top performers carefully evaluate risks and select options that balance potential rewards with safety.
2. **Problem-Solving:** Good decisions allow you to overcome challenges swiftly.
3. **Adaptability:** Being able to make quick, flexible decisions ensures you stay effective, even in changing conditions.

Poor Decision-Making Undermines Performance

1. **Decision Fatigue:** When faced with too many decisions, your mental clarity can suffer—leading to poorer choices.

2. **Emotional and Cognitive Influences:** Stress, pressure, and strong emotions can cloud judgment and you can make poor decisions made under emotional strain.

Overall, developing emotional regulation and clear thinking through tools like mindfulness, self-awareness, or structured decision frameworks can significantly improve both decision making and your life. On a personal note, like many others, I often felt overwhelmed when trying to tackle personal issues or make decisions. It was a classic case of analysis paralysis, something that can impact performance across all areas of life. To manage this, I developed a method I call The Box Approach.

The concept is simple: break down your problems or concerns into separate sections. This helps you sort through your thoughts and emotions more clearly, making it easier to focus on one issue at a time.

When we're juggling too many things at once, everything tends to pile up, and that sense of overwhelm can lead to emotional rather than rational decisions. In those moments, it often feels easier to make a quick mental judgment rather than pause and work things out on paper. But that rush can lead to choices we later regret.

The Box Approach gives you space to view each issue individually, without being consumed by the weight of everything at once. Start by dividing the areas you're concerned about or genuinely want to improve into separate sections.

Here are some examples:

- **Relationships**—with yourself, your partner, family, friends, acquaintances, and more.
- **Work/Career**—challenges with your job, building a career, or finding your path.
- **Finances**—things like emergency savings, retirement planning, budgeting, or investing.
- **Physical Clutter**—material stuff that adds stress, like cars, furniture, or multiple homes.
- **Mental Clutter**—anxiety, worries, endless to-do lists, and racing thoughts.
- **Physical Health**—exercise, sports, losing weight, or simply moving your body regularly

How to Begin the Box Approach

Once you've identified the areas of concern in your life, this is where The Box Approach really begins.

Start by finding a quiet space, free from distractions. Grab a pen and paper, and draw a simple grid like the one below. Label each box with a specific area you're dealing with. This could be work, health, relationships, finances, or anything else relevant to your life. Then assign a number to each box based on its priority. Feel free to add or adjust the boxes to suit your unique situation.

Box Approach

Relationships	**Finances**
Priority 1	*Priority 2*
Work / Career	**Physical Clutter**
Priority 3	*Priority 6*
Mental Clutter	**Physical Health**
Priority 5	*Priority 4*

Step 1: Take a Moment with Each Box

In the order of prioritization, answer the following questions:

1. **What is the issue I'm dealing with?**
   (*Break down the specific problem you're trying to solve.*)

2. **Do I need to make a decision right now?**
   (*Yes or No*)

3. **Am I capable and ready to make this decision?**
   (*Yes or No—explain your answer, considering your current mental, emotional, and physical state.*)

4. **Have I rationally considered all my options?**
   (*Take a moment to assess whether you've truly weighed the pros and cons.*)

Step 2: Explore Possible Options

Now, list out all the possible decisions or actions you could take related to the issue. You answer the same four questions listed above, for each option. Then, evaluate each option using the following criteria and rate them on a scale of 1 to 5:

- **Values:** *Does this option align with my core values?*
- **Knowledge:** *Have I researched this option thoroughly? Do I feel informed?*
- **Effort:** *How much time, energy, or resources will this require from me?*

- **Vision:** *Will this support or hinder the long-term vision I have for my life?*

Scoring:

Add up the scores for each option. A total score between **15 and 20** suggests this is a well-aligned, confident choice that you can feel secure in pursuing.

Step 3: Ground Your Process

These three guiding questions can help shift the decision-making process from being overwhelming to manageable:

- After considering all the options, do you still need more time to make a decision?
- What internal or external factors might be influencing your clarity?
- What adjustments can you make to feel more secure and confident in your decision?

The Box Approach isn't a perfect system and it's certainly not a one-size-fits-all solution. But what it does offer is a structured pause, a moment to reflect, sort through complexity, and build more mindful decision-making habits. It's not about finding the "right" answer or solving everything at once. Rather, it's a tool, a wellness tool, to help slow things down and create space for clarity.

Breaking things down into boxes takes effort. It's a process that requires patience and practice, more like a marathon than a sprint. But through it, I've found a way to tackle challenges without feeling completely overwhelmed or stuck in analysis paralysis. We all make decisions based on the information we have at the time, shaped by our circumstances and what feels safe or necessary at that moment.

In today's fast-paced, tech-driven world, our minds still operate with instincts shaped by a much older time. That's why something as analog and simple as writing things down, box by box, can feel surprisingly grounding. It reconnects us to ourselves and brings a kind of clarity that digital tools often overlook.

If you would like a free copy of the box approach you can get yours by visiting https://maritaespada.com **or scan the QR code below.**

Creating the Box Approach marked the beginning of a deeper personal growth journey. Around twelve years ago, when I first started exploring what personal development actually meant, I didn't have a clear starting point. There was no mentor to guide me, no support group to lean on. I had to figure things out on my own. My only resources were time, a laptop, and an internet connection.

So, I began by studying people who seemed to embody a balance between happiness, fulfillment, and success. Entrepreneurs were my first focus. Immersed in Silicon Valley culture, where startups and hustle culture were everywhere, entrepreneurship felt like the natural entry point. The common narrative was that building something from the ground up would shape not only your career but also your personal life, delivering lessons, purpose, and, eventually, satisfaction.

But after reading story after story of so-called success, I wasn't convinced. The entrepreneurial path didn't seem to hold the answers I was looking for, at least not in the way I needed. That's when I shifted my attention to athletes. I became fascinated by the connection between performance, mindset, and vision. Athletes train for peak performance, driven by a desire to win and push limits. Their focus isn't just physical; it's mental, emotional, and strategic. Their journeys felt more relatable to me. As someone who played sports most of my life, often as a way to cope and escape, it felt more personal and grounded. Through their stories, I began to uncover the early ideas that would later shape what I now call renegade beliefs, the inner convictions that drive people to break molds and commit to their own path, even when it's unconventional.

As I dove deeper into their techniques, training methods, and mental strategies, my curiosity only grew.

I started asking myself:
- How do they create discipline and determination, as they hold on to who they are and their beliefs?
- How do they resist the urge to overthink each move?
- How do they trust that their discipline and preparation will carry them through the season?
- How do they hold onto their vision through setbacks?

These questions became my compass.

Renegade Performance Stories

The story Shawn Green shared in a short TED Talk back in 2012 might have some answers for those questions above. If you take a look at Shawn Green's statistics, they'll show that he was an incredible baseball player who was accepted into the Baseball Hall of Fame. But the data won't show you the journey he went through to get there. His career began on September 28, 1993, when he became the second-youngest player in the major league. He would then go on to play for fifteen seasons with four different teams: the Toronto Blue Jays, the Los Angeles Dodgers, the Arizona Diamondbacks, and the New York Mets.

On a day like any other, his general manager and coach approached him with the idea to change his batting approach. Rather than hitting up the middle, they wanted him to bat to right field, as they thought that this could make a difference in his game. Shawn was a hitter with power potential, and this change would allow him to hit more home runs. He had to trust their approach was the best for him, even though he thought his batting average would suffer. Although he wasn't thrilled, he went along with what they asked him to do. As a result, his performance suffered for years. He explains that this change kept him from being true to himself. His story resonated deeply with me, as for many years I was not true to myself. When we neglect and bury emotions in life, they will manifest within us, and we can end up depressed, in a rut, and unmotivated. Shawn knew his performance was the key indicator of how his baseball career would unfold. If he underperformed, he could be benched or sent back to the minor leagues.

During the offseason, he decided to see a Qigong instructor to get help. Qigong is an ancient Chinese martial meditation that brings together breathing techniques, concentration, and movement exercises. After a few months, he started to feel the positive changes in both his mind and body, and as the next season approached, he thought he was ready, only to find out that he had been benched indefinitely. He approached the general manager and begged for a trade since being benched might label him as a nonstarter and end his baseball career. Out of frustration at the potential idea of losing his baseball career, he decided to go rogue and practice his batting strategy on his own terms. One day, the hitting coach saw him, chased him down, and told him, "The batting cage is off limits for you without my supervision." Shawn couldn't believe it. As he puts it, in an instant his practice had turned into T-ball. He was upset, and his ego kicked in. After he was able to let go of that anger, he embraced the tee thanks to his new Qigong practice.

In a few short weeks, the general manager ordered him back in the lineup. On May 23, after being benched for so long, he had one of his best single performances ever. As he was about to bat, he would repeat, "Chop wood, carry water. Chop wood, carry water."

This mantra allowed him to focus on the work at hand, one goal at a time. That mantra is used in Qigong and other similar practices as a way to pause, embrace, and appreciate the process and the present moment. As a result, he hit four home runs in a single game. Shawn was unapologetically a renegade. He had a vision that no one else could see, and he pushed against the constructs of what his coaches were telling him to do versus what he felt was right, he saw beyond his circumstances.

Through all that, he was able to find his true self as a ball player, and eventually this led him to become a hall-of-fame ball player.

The art of manifestation is also a powerful tool, one that transcends industries, professions, and backgrounds. Actor Jim Carrey is a well-known example of someone who embraced this mindset early in his career. Over the years, Carrey has consistently shown a renegade belief in challenging the norms of fame and the entertainment industry, particularly as he's openly shared his personal struggles with identity and self-worth.

On February 17, 1997, during an appearance on *The Oprah Winfrey Show*, Carrey spoke candidly about the role visualization played in his success. He told the story of how, years earlier, he had written himself a check for $10 million for "acting services rendered," post-dated for Thanksgiving 1995. He carried that check in his wallet for years, even as it began to fall apart. Just before that self-imposed deadline, he landed his breakout role in *Dumb and Dumber* earned, incredibly, $10 million.

Carrey's story is a testament to how powerful visualization can be when combined with action. As he wisely put it during the interview, "You can't just visualize it and then go eat a sandwich." Manifestation isn't magic. It's clarity of vision, paired with hard work, persistence, and belief.

What better example of combining manifestation with disciplined action than legendary athletes like Michael Jordan, Kobe Bryant, and Scottie Pippen? You might ask: what was the common thread behind their peak performance? It wasn't just talent or determination. It was the influence of their renegade coach, Phil Jackson. Phil Jackson's unconventional coaching style elevated these already gifted athletes to an entirely new level. While he had a strong background in basketball, playing through high school and college, it wasn't until college that he experienced what he later called a "rude spiritual awakening," opening his mind to new ways of thinking.

Over time, Jackson came to see peak performance as a fusion of the mind and body. It's not just about telling players to "get your head in the game," it's about how to get your mind into alignment with your body to unlock real power and flow.

During his time coaching the Chicago Bulls in the 1990s, Jackson explored the idea of implementing mindfulness practices with his team, something almost unheard of at the time. Meditation was still considered fringe, associated with "hippie" culture or Eastern mysticism, not professional sports. But Jackson saw potential. He reached out to Jon Kabat-Zinn, a pioneer in mindfulness-based stress reduction, who then introduced him to George Mumford. George a former basketball player who once roomed with the legendary Julius "Dr. J" Erving, brought both credibility and deep understanding to the table. His experience gave him the street cred necessary to connect with NBA stars. Players like Michael Jordan and Kobe Bryant didn't just respect him—they listened. His mindfulness techniques weren't abstract ideas; they were practical tools that led to real results.

Together, Jackson and Mumford integrated mindfulness and meditation into the Bulls' training routines. One of their signature practices was *One Team, One Breath*—a powerful yet simple exercise where players focused on syncing their breathing. Over time, this helped the team enter a collective flow state, where they weren't just individual athletes trying to win, but a unified force, fully present in the moment.

That connection between breath, focus, and teamwork allowed them to transcend pressure and achieve peak performance together.

Phil Jackson, a classic type-A personality, had to learn how to let go of control in order to fully embrace these practices. As a fellow type-A person, I relate deeply. It's hard to release the need to control outcomes or script every move. But Jackson offered a piece of advice that stuck with me: **"You begin your day with a quiet mind, giving up control."**

It's a simple idea with powerful implications, especially for those of us constantly trying to plan, predict, and perfect everything.

Phil Jackson didn't just coach games. He reshaped the mindset of elite athletes. He was, and still is, a renegade coach who stepped outside the traditional playbook to explore tools that no one else dared to use at the time. The result? Multiple championships and a legacy that goes far beyond the court.

Our last renegade performance story can really make us pause, ponder, and realize that although goals are important, because they can make us feel fulfilled, happy, and successful, ignoring the warning signs of burnout can end up costing us more in the long run.

The hustle-and-grind momentum kicked in for Mardy Fish in his late twenties when he realized he hadn't been giving his tennis career his all. He then made a commitment to himself to become one of the top eight players in the world and to participate in the 2011 year-end tournament.

In 2009, Fish reinvented himself, hired a physical trainer that moved in with him and his wife and created a detailed, rigid training cycle. He stopped eating sweets and consuming alcohol and instead hyper-focused on training to achieve greatness as a tennis player. He went to bed early to get plenty of rest and stopped spending time going out with friends to refocus his energy on his commitment. Every game inched him closer and closer to becoming the number one player in the country. Eventually, he achieved that goal and participated in the 2011 end-of-year tour.

One night, as 2012 approached, he woke up with his heart pounding, eventually reaching a rate of 240 beats per minute. When he later described the incident, he said he thought he was going to die. He went to the hospital, where they diagnosed him with a form of arrhythmia and performed a procedure to treat it. In addition, he had a severe anxiety disorder that, as the story goes, later evolved into a much more complicated psychological problem that would require further treatment. As his focus shifted to becoming one of the top ten players in the world, the pressures from the game continued to build.

In 2012 during the US Open, he felt overwhelmed with anxiety on the way to the stadium. As he explained this to his wife, she simply said, "You don't have to play." He could not grasp the idea of not playing. He had been training hard for this exact moment, the moment to play against the greatest of all time, Roger Federer.

He then paused and realized she was right. "I don't have to play." The game was called off, and this kicked off months of Fish staying home, tormented with a severe anxiety disorder. With the help of a psychiatrist, he worked through it with meditations and managing the narratives in his head. He has not overcome his anxiety disorder, but he has learned to live with it. As he speaks about his experience, he hopes he can help others with his story. His anxiety was so overwhelming that the place he loved the most became the place that triggered his anxiety, and he was not self-aware enough to recognize what his body was telling him.

He has since retired to focus on his mental health journey, and he's found a competitive outlet in the game of golf; he competes in the celebrity golf circuit.

Fish was a renegade in a time when mental health was not a consideration in the sports arena. He brought it to the forefront and broke down barriers for others, allowing young athletes to be open about mental struggles, and learn how to balance their ambitious goals with their own anxieties.

As I read, watched, and listened to these renegade stories, I came to realize that what I was really missing was that sweet balance between performance, making good decisions, and holding it all together through emotional regulation. No one taught me how to do this. To be honest, most of us aren't taught. Through my journals, I saw that, starting as young as thirteen, I spent many years trying to piece it all together.

Here is a journal clipping from 2006: "The things that scare us the most are the ones worthwhile in the end."

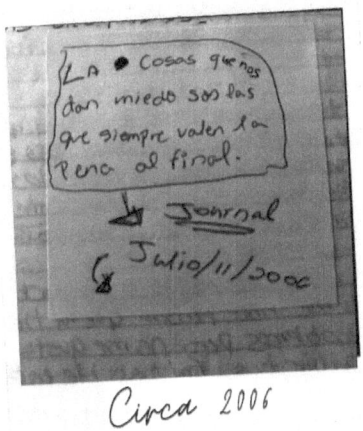

Circa 2006

In 2006, during my college years, I was training my mind to take risks, but not calculated risks. During my first year in San Francisco, I attempted to change that.

After reading these renegade stories for yourself, what chapters of your own life or moments are you currently living that connect to these themes of performance and growth?

For me, the stories I just shared left me with one open question: How can we recognize our limitations and use them as leverage to live a bigger, fuller life?

After reading these renegade stories for yourself, what chapters of your own life or moments are you currently living that connect to these themes of performance and growth?

For me, the stories I just shared left me with one open question: How can we recognize our limitations and use them as leverage to live a bigger, a fuller life?

Managing Our Limitations

Learning to recognize your own limitations gets a lot easier when you practice being present just taking things moment by moment when you practice mindfulness. Real growth happens when you give yourself permission to open all those mental doors and take an honest look at what's inside even the thoughts emotions or memories that feel a little uncomfortable. But here's the thing you can't do any of that unless you're actually open to the experience.

Which reminds me of this Buddhist parable, that conveys this message clearly with the story of a simple cup of tea. There was a Japanese Zen master named Nan-in who lived during the Meiji era (1868–1912).

During his days as a teacher, he was visited by a university professor curious about Zen.

Nan-in served tea. He poured his visitor's cup full, then kept on pouring. The professor watched the overflow until he could no longer restrain himself. "It is overfull. No more will go in!"

"Like this cup," Nan-in said, "you are full of your own opinions and speculations. How can I show you Zen unless you first empty your cup?"

We can't truly embrace different opinions, perspectives, or experiences if we're too full of our own. Our minds are shaped in ways we don't always realize: by upbringing, culture, habit, and repetition. But like any muscle, the mind can be trained, stretched, and expanded.

In the mindfulness meditation sessions I lead, one of the most powerful exercises is something I call Working with Perspectives. After everyone settles into a seated position, we begin with a few deep breaths, grounding ourselves in the present moment. Once the group feels centered, I ask them to visualize "the world." I don't give any hints or prompts, just the simple phrase: visualize the world.

When the chimes ring to signal the end of the session, we come together and share what we saw. Some people picture Earth floating in space. Others imagine a bustling city filled with strangers. Some think of their families or their childhood homes. Every image is unique. Every "world" is different.

That's the point of the exercise: to show how even when we hear the same exact words, our minds interpret them through deeply personal filters. We all have different reference points, beliefs, and emotional landscapes. And no matter how strongly we believe in our own view, we can't force someone else to see things the same way. Sometimes we can negotiate or find common ground, but sometimes we can't. Recognizing this is essential, especially in personal and professional relationships. It's a limitation we all live with, and one we must learn to manage with empathy and patience.

In moments when emotions run high and perspectives clash, often what your body needs most is something simple: a breath. Deep breathing sends a calming message to your nervous system, helping you move out of survival mode and into clarity. Pairing your breath with a mantra, a few grounding words, can also help quiet anxious thought patterns.

A mantra doesn't have to be complicated. It can be short and sweet, or a little longer if that feels right. One I've personally used often is: *"Nothing to win, nothing to lose."* It reminds me not to take things too seriously and helps dismantle the fears I sometimes build up in my own head. Feel free to borrow it, or create your own words that speak to you.

When we're overwhelmed, our bodies often fall into one of the four common stress responses: fight, flight, freeze, or fawn.

Each one is rooted in survival instincts, and each presents differently:

- **Fight** mode feels like intense anger or the urge to lash out. Your heart races, blood pressure rises, and your focus narrows.
- **Flight** kicks in when you feel like running away or avoiding a situation altogether. You might feel panicked or desperate to escape.
- **Freeze.** The shutdown response is your body goes still, your breath becomes shallow, and you may feel disconnected or numb.
- **Fawn.** It is a lesser-known response but just as real. It often shows up in people who prioritize others' needs above their own, those who say yes when they want to say no, avoid conflict, and struggle to set boundaries.

These are all natural reactions, especially for those who've experienced trauma. But they don't have to control us. With self-awareness, mindfulness, and consistent inner work, we can learn to recognize our patterns and respond in healthier, more intentional ways.

Back in 2005, I experienced firsthand what it feels like when your body's stress response goes into overdrive. That was the year I found the courage to come out as gay to my family and friends. I was nineteen, overwhelmed by anxiety, nerves, and a fear I couldn't quite name. Every part of me felt on edge—my body had gone straight into fight-or-flight mode.

At the time, I was secretly dating a woman who was much older than me. No one knew. That summer, my cousin Tina and her girlfriend Gee came to visit us in Puerto Rico from Miami. They were staying at my mom's house, and one night, after a typical summer time dinner, Gee and I decided to go to Blockbuster to rent a movie for everyone.

Blockbuster, with its soft glow and nostalgic charm, felt oddly calming. The quiet buzz of CRT TVs playing previews, the occasional beep from the checkout counter, the distant soundtrack from whatever film was on the overhead screens, it was all so familiar. And yet, I was about to change my life forever.

Somewhere between the aisles and the popcorn-scented air, I blurted it out. I told Gee I was gay. She was the first person in my family to know. I don't remember exactly how I said it, but I remember how I felt: worried and relieved all at once.

The next day, Tina and Gee encouraged me to tell the rest of the family. They smiled in that knowing way, as if to say, They probably already know. It's okay. Still, I hesitated. Saying it out loud to more people felt like leaping off a cliff. But deep down, I knew that the longer I stayed silent, the more that silence would eat away at me.

A few weeks later, a package arrived in the mail from them, wrapped in soft green paper tied with a neat bow. Inside was a DVD of the movie *Imagine Me and You*. In the movie, Rachel is walking down the aisle when she spots a woman named Luce in the crowd and feels an immediate, powerful connection. It's love at first sight. The two quickly become close friends, and when Rachel discovers that Luce is a lesbian, she begins to question her own feelings and identity. Despite being happily married, Rachel finds herself falling for Luce, facing the difficult choice between her marriage and this thrilling new romance.

As I watched the movie for the first time, I realized that I didn't want to live a secret life, that doing so would cause me more harm. I didn't want to look back at my life years later and think of what could have been because I hid who I was from everyone around me.

Eventually, I made my way to my grandfather's house to tell my aunt. After what felt like the longest drive of my life, I climbed the three red matte quarry steps leading to the front door and walked straight to her bedroom. Standing there, I hesitated before saying, "Umm, I don't really know how to say this... I'm gay." She didn't seem surprised. She gave me a warm hug and nodded toward my grandfather's office, encouraging me to tell him next.

As I entered his office, he was focused on paperwork, with classical music softly playing in the background. Without really thinking, I blurted it out. I don't even remember my exact words. He looked up briefly, said little, then looked back down and opened a drawer in his desk. "I know," he said quietly. "I always knew." Then he pulled out some yellowed newspaper clippings he had saved years ago, articles about advocates across the island working to support gay children. I took the papers as a tear rolled down my cheek.

I had been so worried that he would think less of me even though I had adored him and loved him so much.

After I left my grandfather's office, my aunt suggested we drive back to my mom's house to tell her. When we arrived, my mom was surprised to see us, but as we sat together in the living room, I told her. She hugged me and said she would always love me. Over time, my family acted like their love and acceptance were unconditional, that no matter what, I'd be safe with them. But deep down, I still didn't feel secure.

A few months later, my mom voiced her confusion, wondering aloud how this could have happened—how I was gay, and how I had become gay. She hinted that maybe it was because she had let me play sports and do things that "girls shouldn't" do. Her words made me worry for months that once they fully processed everything, they might see me as a monster. I kept having flashbacks to the rumors I faced in high school, what happened to Cynthia, Jorge, and others around me who had come out and probably felt the same fight-flight-freeze-fawn responses.

You've probably heard about the inner critic—the voice inside that judges us. Sometimes it's triggered by real situations, setting off our fight-or-flight response. Other times, it's that inner critic taking control and stirring up those feelings even when there's no real threat. This is natural; it's how we evolved. The problem is, in today's world, we're rarely chased by lions, yet the inner critic still acts like it's protecting us from immediate danger.

We are unable to stop the inner critic, but we learn to work with it. A few years ago, I watched a Ted Talk called "The Most Important Lesson from 83,000 Brain Scans." Two sentences from it stand out to me: "Behavior is not the problem. Behavior is an expression of the problem." We often become victims of our circumstances, our experiences, and even our inner critic. This is how our behavior becomes an expression of the problem, and that is why working on healing the expression of the problem can be key.

There is a Buddhist parable, the second arrow, that explains how we become victims of our circumstances. It's explained that when you experience someone saying or doing something that might annoy or upset you, that becomes the first arrow. You are hurt, and in managing that painful experience, your reaction becomes the second arrow. It's this rush of emotions and feelings that have little to no connection to the first arrow. At times the second arrow, which is launched by ourselves to ourselves, is even more hurtful than the first.

But how can we manage the pain of this second arrow? How can we identify when this might happen? For me, this has been an unending internal battle, the impulsive behaviors that intensified most of my suffering.

To be honest, our inner critic, our self-chatter, that guy is a total jackass. Not only would this voice get me in trouble, but when I fed it, I ended up doing reckless things. With time, I started to find ways to stop feeding the jackass inside me and things started to unfold for the better. A lighter side emerged along with it, and a new mindset started to peel open.

Working With Mindsets

Your mindset is the lens through which you view the world; it has the power to shape how you experience everything around you. Take something as simple as a sunset: one person might see it as a symbol of loss, the close of yet another day, while someone else may see it as a promise that tomorrow holds new beauty. For years, my mindset was fixed; I couldn't adjust it even if I wanted to. I was so consumed by my surroundings that it didn't seem like I had any control. My circumstances felt so overwhelming that the idea of changing them seemed completely ridiculous to me. Our mindset influences how we interpret the world and respond to it. Imagine your mindset as a box containing your attitudes, opinions, and judgments. Everything you believe and feel about a situation lives inside that box. As the seasons change, so does your mindset and I've found that taking time to reevaluate my mindset with the changing seasons can help me stay grounded.

Every time a new season comes, I consider these three things:
- What drains me?
- What restores me?
- How are my goal systems working?

Items I consider draining include:
- Too much social media
- Sleeping too little
- Spending time with people who might be negative and do not align with many of my values.

Items that I have listed as restorative are:
- Meditation
- Sleeping eight hours
- A hot shower
- Sitting outside with a coffee or tea

- Playing with my dog
- Having date night with my wife

It's best to focus on the path to achieving the goal instead of the goal itself. The end results can be better if we focus on the seeds we are planting and nurturing the process, instead of focusing on the result from the start.

For example, let's say your goal is to become more financially responsible. Rather than constantly checking your bank account and feeling discouraged, you can focus on building healthy financial habits. Create a budget, pause before making big purchases, and practice being more intentional with your spending. The aim isn't to become the next Warren Buffett; it's to develop a sustainable, mindful approach to managing your money.

The best way to think of this system is to allow your goals to shape the person you would like to be, rather than using goals to define the person that you are.

Additional Questions and Journal Prompts to Help Shape and Define Your Mindset

- How would you describe your relationship with self-honesty? Is there a truth within you that you're ready to explore, write about, or begin releasing?

- What is your current relationship with yourself? Are you making space for self-care? Are you allowing yourself to fully accept where you are on your journey right now?

There is something to be said about taking a pen and paper and giving power to the words you write and letting go as you do so. It's the action of putting those thoughts on paper and reviewing them, where we can really see our level of growth and even healing. I use every new season as a way to renew commitments and promises I make to myself or create new commitments to the person I want to be.

One recent commitment I've made is to be more mindful of the people I choose to spend my time with. While it can be fun to surround myself with those who live for the moment, I've come to realize that not every social gathering supports my personal growth. Some relationships, though enjoyable, can become distractions, pulling my focus and energy away from what truly matters to me. If we're not intentional, these connections can quietly shape our inner dialogue, influence our mindset, and color the way we experience the world.

If you'd like a free copy of the Mindful Renegade Journal Prompts, visit https://maritaespada.com
or simply scan the QR code below.

Radical Compassion

Radical compassion is the act of putting in the effort to educate yourself about empathy, not only understanding your own feelings but also recognizing and honoring what others may be experiencing. The ability to hold and appreciate two different perspectives simultaneously can be a radical act, especially because it's often very challenging to do. With that in mind, many people find not only meaning but also compassion through spirituality.

Throughout the years I found meaning in Secular Buddhism. Over the years, I found meaning in Secular Buddhism. At first, it was hard to put into words. Even talking about Secular Buddhism and Radical Compassion felt unfamiliar and almost strange. Showing myself grace and compassion seemed like a sign of weakness, and maybe it still does to some people. But life and everything in it can be taken far too seriously. This perspective helped me avoid falling into that trap, and it can help you too.

And let's be honest, personal growth and self-care come with their fair share of awkward moments and laughs along the way.

Secular Buddhism can be seen as a grassroots movement aimed at reinterpreting Buddhism through a rational, secular lens. It is not a religion but a path centered primarily on meditation practice. Through Secular Buddhism, I learned even more about the practice of meditation, which opened many doors for me. It has the ability to bring your mind and body together for a moment in time. The two are dancing to a different rhythm throughout the day, stepping on each other's toes. We have a to-do list involving personal items, work, and family, and in the background our minds are stressing about balancing them all.

Many people, including myself, begin meditation sessions curious about what mindfulness can do for us. Often, beginners hope for a sudden awakening through meditation, but I would argue that this expectation is misguided. Rather than triggering an instant revelation, meditation primarily heightens our sensory awareness. Basic guided meditations typically focus on the breath, bodily sensations, or visual imagery.

In real-life situations, emotions deeply interact with our sensory system. For example, when you feel anger, you might notice your face growing warm, your heart racing, or your hands trembling. Often, by the time you recognize your anger, you've already embraced it and reacted. Meditation teaches us to notice and label these emotions and sensations before responding. This awareness allows us to unpack our reactions and ultimately improve how we experience life.

When I began my own meditation journey, I learned the fundamentals from experienced practitioners who had been at it for decades. One important lesson I've embraced is that while action is sometimes necessary, sometimes the best choice is inaction. We don't need to respond to everything immediately; pausing before acting can often lead to better outcomes.

In one of those lessons, I became more familiar with the mindfulness practice called RAIN. As someone who struggles to have empathy for myself, it has really helped me find kindness and grace for myself at times when self-loathing would otherwise become unbearable. It's a way of bringing compassion to difficult moments or emotions. We have been taught, or told, not to show negative emotions, but healthy emotional regulation is not about ignoring or avoiding them, it's about learning how to process them.

The basis of this technique is to stay aware of your surroundings, thoughts, and feelings and allow them to be here without judgment.

Some have explained this mindfulness exercise as a way to expand our self-awareness. RAIN is an acronym, the four letters standing for

- Recognize
- Allow
- Investigate
- Nurture

Recognize

Take a step back and recognize what is happening and what emotions, thoughts or feelings you are currently experiencing. Consciously acknowledge what might be happening. You could be upset at your boss or your situation. You may even feel powerless. What do you recognize?

Allow

The next step is allowing your situation to be what it is. You can even repeat to yourself, "Right now, it's like this." Sit with your current circumstances, feelings, emotions, and thoughts.

Typically, when we have an unpleasant experience, we react in one of three ways: by piling on judgment or criticism; by numbing ourselves to our feelings, emotions, or thoughts; or by focusing our attention elsewhere. Our ability to pause to do inner work with this experience is what Allow is all about: being able to be present in this raw moment.

Investigate

At this stage you investigate that raw experience or emotion with genuine interest and curiosity. Ask yourself questions to dive deeper into it. How did this start? Have I felt this way before? What do I need to do? It's a way for you to understand the nature of your thoughts and actions, including thoughts of yourself, with an open mind and full open awareness.

Nurture

This final stage represents the choice to not identify yourself with your negative experiences. It's about coming to a place of knowing that they are small, fleeting aspects of the totality that you are. We must be aware and understand that these emotions, feelings, and thoughts are felt in our mind and body because of external factors managed by our sensory inputs.

I see this exercise much like tending a garden. The moment you stop pulling the weeds, they quickly overrun the beautiful plants you've nurtured with such care. It's a delicate process for everyone. By tending to our mental garden, clearing away the weeds, we create space for growth and beauty to flourish. In doing so, we're offering ourselves the profound gift of radical compassion and radical love.

Take your time and explore RAIN as a standalone meditation or consider moving through the steps whenever challenging feelings arise.

In addition to RAIN, I created my own acronym, **MIND**, that provides a space between intense moments. This one is just a simple word that I repeat in my meditation practices:

- **Mindfulness:** Practice it daily.
- **Intentional:** Be intentional with your life.
- **No:** Say no when you need to.
- **Day-by Day:** Live in the moment.

These reminders can be extremely helpful, and you could even create your own acronym to lean on when needed.

When we're young, we're constantly wrestling with our own identities, trying to find ourselves within a vast forest of ideals. Our emotions and bodies are still developing, which means our decision-making often falls short of wisdom. As we grow older, we draw closer to our North Star—gaining clarity on who we want to be and how to live authentically as that person. Being a renegade means living in alignment with your values, a process that takes dedication and effort. The RAIN exercise can help navigate that same forest, guiding you toward where you want to be when you're ready to arrive. Mindfulness isn't about silencing the busy mind; it's about transforming the way we relate to it.

To support this practice, I use a simple digital tool, a note-taking app, to create a "brain dump." Whenever worries or tasks arise, I jot them down, clearing my mind once they're recorded. From there, I prioritize and manage these items over days, weeks, or months. This not only opens mental space to focus on what truly matters but also creates a practical, strategic way to handle life's demands. Spiritually, it helps me feel less cluttered inside, while practically, it's a plan to stay grounded amid chaos.

I've come to understand that mental health is a continuous journey, not a race with a finish line. It's about regularly checking in with ourselves, offering grace when we stumble, and embracing the courage to begin again without judgment. Ultimately, it's about giving ourselves permission to cultivate radical compassion because if I can't cut myself some slack for binge-watching an entire season in one night, what's even the point of self-care?

A Scientific Twist

On my own mental health journey, I have researched and even worked with professionals to heal myself from the inside out. Through different therapy sessions, I have been treated with brain spotting, breathwork, medications, you name it. The one thing that I learned on my own that helped me put this puzzle together was the study of brain waves.

In short, you want to stimulate beta waves for tackling challenging mental tasks, delta waves to promote deep sleep, and theta waves to enter a deep, trance-like state during meditation.

Brain waves were never something I gave much thought to. The term often felt like a buzzword, something people tossed around after reading about it in a book, just to spice up a dinner conversation. I came to realize that the more we learn about brain waves, the deeper our understanding of the mind and its complexity becomes. I discovered how factors like exercise, meditation, diet, and the levels of dopamine and serotonin can influence us. Brain waves play a vital role because they impact our emotions, thoughts, and overall mental well-being.

Our brains emit brain waves when a group of neurons sends electrical pulses to another group of neurons. These wavelike patterns align with one of the five types listed below:

- **Gamma.** These are what everyone would like to achieve on a daily basis. They're associated with heightened perception, learning, and problem-solving tasks. Gamma waves indicate interactions between different regions of the brain.

- **Beta.** These arise from alertness, normal consciousness, or active thinking. They are related to focused tasks, such as having a conversation and actively listening.

- **Alpha.** This one is interesting, as studies have shown that an increase of alpha waves can help with depression. These waves can increase our ability to digest new information and increase creativity.

- **Theta.** These can occur with reduced consciousness, such as deep relaxation.

- **Delta.** These are the waves that we might experience as restorative sleep in a dreamless state.

Our environment, sleep, healthy habits, stress, anxiety, and productivity can influence how our brain waves evolve throughout the day. Breathing, not only brings life to our body, but is also a tool to balance our minds when change strikes unexpectedly. When things feel overwhelming, I know I need to break the narrative that is making me spiral.

To do this, I practice the 3 × 3 Breath Exercise. This is a simple exercise that allows us to take a step back and see the bigger picture.

- Close your eyes.
- Name an object around you.
- Take a deep breath and exhale slowly.
- Repeat the process above three times.

You may find many similar exercises that provide the same pattern-breaking benefits.

As a final resource for this chapter, I've created a curated playlist for you. While some tracks are simply great tunes, others are designed to stimulate specific brain waves. Over time, I've used music to enhance focus, spark creativity, and promote restful sleep. Think of it as the book's unofficial soundtrack, a meaningful companion and a fun extra.

Research shows that music therapy can be profoundly healing and has been used to support a wide range of conditions. I personally learned more about the power of music therapy when my father was hospitalized, fighting for his life. Beyond

Western medicine, music was also used to support his healing journey, showing me firsthand how music can be a powerful aid in recovery.

More of this story unfolds ahead...

You can find my playlist on Spotify as
"A Renegade's Journey to Stillness Book"
or you can scan the QR below

3

THE INNER RENEGADE AND CONTEMPLATIVE PRACTICES

Many people are alive but don't touch the miracle of being alive.
—THÍCH NHẤT HẠNH

One contemplative practice that I have embraced, as I've mentioned, is mindfulness meditation. No seriously, meditation helped with my ADHD. I just need to explain it...oh look, a bird. I will be forever grateful for it. This practice of mindfulness has allowed me to shift my perspective about life in general. However, it hasn't solved every issue in my life; it isn't a one-size-fits-all cure for mental health issues. I still have to wake up every day and work hard to prevent old patterns from finding their way back to me.

I used to see life as a marathon, one I had to finish before anyone else. Though it's a long race, I thought that my speed and accuracy would allow me to reach the finish line first. I carried a constant sense of urgency, as if time were slipping away and I needed to reach some undefined destination. It felt like I was racing to complete a masterpiece, always searching for the missing piece that would make it whole.

But over time, I began to understand that the masterpiece isn't a final product; it's the journey itself. It's shaped by the lessons we collect along the way, both big and small. We often fixate on major milestones, believing they're the only moments that matter, and in doing so, we overlook everything in between. I know I did. I missed the beauty in the ordinary, the quiet moments, the daily rituals, the love woven into everyday life. It took time, but I've come to see that those small, often overlooked details are what truly give life its depth and meaning. And of course, a taco or ice cream at the end of a busy day doesn't hurt either.

How many times have you truly paused today? How often did you close your eyes, even for a moment, to offer your mind a bit of stillness?

If your answer is none, you're not alone. That's the nature of modern life, constantly racing against time, chasing tasks, deadlines, and the next thing on the list. We're always moving, rarely stopping, as if stillness were a luxury we can't afford.

The ability to sit and meditate has allowed me to pause, zoom out, and see the bigger picture. Even in the most difficult times, when my mind is racing, when the feeling of overwhelm can easily take the driver's seat, I make myself pause, stop the race, and just sit.

When people talk about meditation or mindfulness, it's often linked to spiritual traditions or conjures images of someone sitting cross-legged, barefoot, and wrapped in a shawl atop a quiet mountain. But the truth is, meditators are just as likely to be wearing power suits as they are robes. They're politicians, executives, and professionals navigating the chaos of high-stress environments.

There's a common myth that only those who appear calm, collected, and serene are qualified to teach meditation. In reality, the most valuable teachers are often those who've lived through both extremes, stress and stillness, and can guide others from the depth of their own experience.

One respected meditation teacher used to challenge his students to meditate while listening to the news. The idea wasn't to escape discomfort, but to practice remaining grounded in the midst of it, to build the mental and emotional muscle memory needed to stay present, even when the world feels overwhelming.

Mindfulness meditation is a powerful tool for enriching your overall experience of life. In this chapter, I'll share how incorporating a contemplative practice transformed my own journey and how it can support yours as well. Together, we'll explore how meditation led me toward stillness, how it can be used as a practical life tool, and how it might find a place in your daily routine.

Even if you've tried meditation before, I invite you to follow along. You might be surprised by what you discover. Mindfulness meditation helps us strengthen essential mental skills like concentration, focus, and equanimity, the ability to stay present without becoming overwhelmed or overly reactive to life's challenges.

Think of mindfulness as a gym for your mind. Just like physical exercise improves our bodies, a regular mindfulness practice supports mental and emotional well-being. A little daily practice can go a long way toward building a more grounded, resilient, and fulfilling life.

Of all the core elements of meditation, **equanimity** is the one that resonates with me most deeply, perhaps because it's also the most challenging for me to cultivate. Living with ADHD, I often find my mind pulled in many directions at once. But practicing equanimity has helped me develop greater awareness of my current state without becoming overwhelmed by it.

It's important to clarify that equanimity isn't about resignation or indifference. The dictionary defines it as "evenness of temper," but it goes deeper than that. It's about staying grounded in the present, able to take meaningful action in your life without being emotionally shaken by your current circumstances. Equanimity is the capacity to meet life exactly as it is.

A meditation teacher once offered a powerful example during a retreat. We were discussing those times in life when stress, anxiety, or worry feels all-consuming, when even meditation seems like it might not help us. The teacher gently said, "Right now we are here. Let's make space for it." He wasn't suggesting we simply accept suffering and move on. Instead, he was encouraging us to fully feel what was present, to hold it, witness it, and then move forward with intention. Equanimity helps us release the additional suffering we often place on top of our pain through resistance, denial, or judgment.

It's the ability to hold both the pleasant and the unpleasant in a kind of masterful balance. I often imagine it like a tightrope walker in a circus, steadily moving back and forth with the same quiet strength and focus, no matter what's beneath them.

I picture equanimity like this:

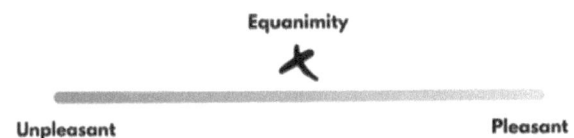

Equanimity allows us to not be pushed and pulled in all directions.

We can begin to cultivate equanimity through our meditation practice and gradually carry it into our daily lives. But striving for equanimity can sometimes feel like climbing a mountain, especially because of something known as **negativity bias**, our brain's natural tendency to focus more on the negative than the positive.

This bias has deep evolutionary roots. For our ancestors, being constantly alert to potential threats was essential for survival. Their heightened sensitivity to danger helped them avoid harm and stay alive in a world full of risks.

But in today's modern world, where most of us aren't facing life or death threats on a daily basis, this bias can become more of a burden than a benefit. It causes us to instinctively give more weight to what's wrong rather than what's going well, tipping the emotional scales toward stress, worry, and fear, even when there's no immediate danger.

By recognizing this built-in tendency, we can begin to shift our perspective. Through mindfulness and meditation, we can train ourselves to notice the full picture, both the good and the bad, and move toward a more balanced, steady presence. That's the heart of equanimity.

The bad news? Negativity bias is hardwired into our brains. The good news? We're not powerless against it. With consistent practice, we can learn to recognize it, regulate it, and even re-shape how we respond to the world around us.

Mindfulness meditation is one of the most effective tools for doing just that. It helps us become more aware of our thought patterns and gives us the space to respond rather than react—especially when we're faced with negativity. Research shows that just eight weeks of regular meditation can lead to significant improvements in how we process information. It also enhances focus, concentration, empathy, gratitude, and more.

In other words, while we may not be able to erase the bias, we can train our minds to see with more balance, clarity, and compassion.

As I began noticing real changes in my brain and mindset, my curiosity deepened. I wanted to understand why this trans-formation was happening. That's when I discovered the concept of neuroplasticity—the brain's incredible ability to adapt, rewire, and change throughout our lives.

For a long time, scientists believed that this kind of flexibil-ity only existed in childhood. We've all heard the phrase "kids' brains are like sponges," often followed by the assumption that adult brains are fixed or less capable of change. And yet, the say-ing, "You can't teach an old dog new tricks," turns out to be more myth than fact.

While it's true that some cognitive functions, like working memory or quick decision-making, may decline slightly with age, our capacity to learn, grow, and form new neural pathways never really disappears.

Meditation plays a powerful role in supporting neuroplasticity. It strengthens focus, enhances memory, and sharpens decision-making. In short, it helps keep the brain agile, responsive, and open to change—no matter your age.

I've often heard people say, "I don't need to meditate, my brain gets a break when I sleep." Well, my friend, that's a common misconception. In reality, your brain doesn't take the night off. While you sleep, it's hard at work, clearing out toxins, consolidating memories, and performing essential maintenance. It's more like a night shift than a rest. Sleep is vital, but it's not the same as giving your mind intentional stillness during waking hours.

Your brain is one of the most important and energy-hungry organs in your body, using up to 20% of your daily energy. Yet we rarely give it the care and attention it deserves. That's where meditation comes in.

Another myth? That you have to stop your thoughts entirely to meditate correctly. The truth is, the mind is meant to think. It's doing what it's designed to do. The goal of meditation isn't to silence your mind, but to notice when your attention drifts and gently bring it back. This act of returning again and again is the practice itself.

Your anchor might be your breath, the sensation of your body against a chair, the tingling in your hands, or a sound in the room. Whatever it is, you return to it. And that simple act trains your brain in presence, patience, and awareness, no silence required.

Building a daily meditation habit has helped me do something I once thought was impossible: change my own mind. In my twenties and early thirties, I truly believed I was destined to live as a tightly wound ball of anger, quietly and consistently sabotaging my own life. I assumed happiness, if it ever showed up, would only visit briefly before slipping away again.

What I didn't realize then was that my anger had roots planted in both past and present experiences, shaped by how I was seen by family, teachers, and even strangers. I wasn't just angry for no reason; I was carrying years of unexamined pain.

Through meditation, I've experienced quiet yet profound shifts in how I think, respond, and navigate the world. These changes didn't arrive with fanfare, but they're deeply real. I find myself laughing more fully, appreciating the small, often overlooked moments. Life feels lighter, more spacious.

My relationships, too, have transformed. While my circle may be smaller now, it feels more intentional. I focus on nurturing connections that are genuine and grounded in authenticity, relationships that reflect the peace I'm learning to cultivate within myself.

Meditation has become such a meaningful part of my life that I now both practice and teach it daily. While I wholeheartedly recommend making it a consistent habit, that doesn't mean it's off-limits when you're simply feeling anxious or overwhelmed. Think of it as another tool in your mental health toolbox— something you can reach for when you need it most.

In fact, meditation can function like a kind of emotional first-aid kit. Even just a few slow, intentional breaths can help you pause, reset, and navigate whatever challenge you're facing. These brief moments of stillness lay the groundwork for deeper practice over time.

Starting small, with just five or ten minutes a day, can help build the mental muscle you need to eventually make meditation a steady part of your daily rhythm. The real power lies not in perfection, but in practice.

Meditation is much like going to the gym regularly—it's a practice that strengthens your mind over time. It can bring calm in moments of anxiety, whether you're about to board a plane or preparing for a big presentation. The true benefits, however, show up more in how you live your daily life than just during the time you spend sitting in meditation. The biggest lesson meditation has taught me is how to prevent my mind from taking over the narrative of my life.

We live in a world full of distractions. Social media pulls us in to see what others are doing, leading to endless comparisons that drain the compassion right out of us. Suddenly, we're wondering, "What if?" instead of embracing the hot mess that is our own journey. And if you're still figuring out how to adult without burning your morning toast, that's okay too.

Today, finding even a few quiet moments alone is rare, and facing our own thoughts can feel overwhelming. I remember being in my early twenties when silence felt frightening. It became such a source of anxiety that I started sleeping with the TV on, which only harmed my sleep. But those quiet moments are important. They help us uncover hidden feelings and emotions we might otherwise avoid. Through healing, we become better versions of ourselves, for both ourselves and those around us. Meditation opens a path toward self-discovery and peace.

Understanding your mind is deeper than most people realize. We often think of self-care as either mental or physical, but they are deeply connected. Listening to our bodies can help us change mental patterns and behaviors.

Some wonder if meditation conflicts with religious beliefs. While meditation has roots in religion, it has evolved into a secular practice embraced by many. It's a tool available to all, regardless of faith.

At a meditation retreat, my teacher once gave me advice that stuck: "Just be simple and easy." I expected a long, profound explanation, but sometimes a few simple words carry more wisdom than a whole book. This isn't about accepting everything as it is, but about letting go of endless worry. Our minds often imagine worst-case scenarios or fears that likely will never happen. This simple mantra can bring ease when your mind spirals out of control.

Perspective shapes how we experience life through our values, experiences, and circumstances. In my twenties and early thirties, I allowed my past to dictate my present and future, letting my mind rule me. As Dr. Gabor Maté said, "We don't respond to what happens. We respond to our perception of what happens."

The pressures of work, responsibilities, and daily life often trigger these reactions. That same pressure can make us forget that our time here isn't unlimited. While life is finite, we can create endless opportunities to learn and truly enjoy the journey.

If you're ready to begin your meditation practice, and not just nap with your eyes closed, I invite you to check out my simple mindfulness meditation in the Insight Timer library under the name Marita Espada. It's guided, calming, and won't judge you if your mind wanders to snacks halfway through.

A direct link to this practice
can also be found on https://maritaespada.com
or the QR code below:

THE FREQUENCY OF HAPPINESS

There is no way to happiness,
happiness is the way.
—Thích Nhất Hanh

What is happiness, really? No, seriously, I'm asking you. Yes, you, the reader. Throughout history, humanity has been on a relentless quest to find it and all the joy it promises. Yet, in that pursuit, we often end up disappointed because happiness is too often framed as an elusive, intangible destination just out of reach.

For much of my life, I felt a constant, almost uncontrollable urge to find purpose and meaning to feel less lost, less alone, and to grow more comfortable in my own skin. In many ways, I was chasing a kind of emotional relief, riding the highs of dopamine and endorphins in search of fleeting happiness. And while those chemical rushes can offer temporary joy, they aren't the key to lasting fulfillment.

Between 2012 and 2013, I was doing my best to elevate my sense of happiness, but I couldn't quite grasp what that actually meant. It felt like a mountain too steep to climb, one I was sure I'd fall short of. I kept struggling with the idea of happiness: how to define it, how to measure it, and how to hold onto it long enough that I wouldn't have to chase it again.

Of course, it wasn't that easy or remotely possible. Some mornings, I'd wake up energized and ready to keep pursuing what felt like an unreachable goal: landing a job in San Francisco. Other mornings, even getting out of bed to sift through job listings felt daunting, and a sense of complete unhappiness would take over. As much as I tried to stay optimistic, deep down, I feared I would never actually live out the dream of moving to Silicon Valley. I've wrestled with happiness and contentment throughout my life, but during that chapter, the struggle felt especially sharp, constant, loud, and unrelenting. So much so that I made many notes throughout my journals, but I didn't really dive into this search for clarity until later.

What I didn't yet understand, something many of us wrestle with, is the distinction between passion and purpose and how that can affect happiness.. At that point in my life, I hadn't clearly defined either. Passion is deeply emotional; it's the spark, the excitement, the connection to what lights you up. Purpose, on the other hand, is rooted in meaning. It's the why behind what you do. Passion can fuel the journey, but purpose gives it direction. Understanding that difference changed everything for me.

If you dive into the research or talk with doctors, you'll find that happiness is often linked to a healthy routine, things like consistent sleep, a balanced work life rhythm, and practices like gratitude and positive thinking. But studies have shown that happiness is more complex than just following a checklist. It's layered, nuanced, and deeply personal, shaped by biology, environment, mindset, and the meaning we attach to our experiences.

In exploring the science of happiness, have we truly considered how individuals perceive risk, specifically the difference between risk aversion and risk management? This isn't to suggest that those who take fewer risks are doomed to miss out on happiness. Rather, it's an invitation to dig deeper, especially as we unpack performance further, as discussed in an earlier chapter, and examine how decision-making and risk tolerance intersect.

Why do some people lean into risk more readily than others? What influences that mindset? And perhaps more importantly, can embracing calculated risks actually lead to greater happiness? These are the questions that help us understand how our approach to uncertainty shapes not just our outcomes, but our overall well-being.

A 2019 study by Northwestern Mutual, titled the "Planning and Progress Study," revealed that the average American has a relatively conservative approach to financial risk, scoring just 4.9 out of 10 on the risk tolerance scale. But the findings didn't stop at finances. The study went further, exploring how people approach risk in other areas of their lives. It examined whether individuals tend to choose the comfort of familiarity, a safer, more predictable path, not just with money, but in personal decisions, relationships, and lifestyle choices. The results point to a broader pattern of risk aversion that extends well beyond the bank account.

The results were interesting:

- 65 percent of people studied preferred the consistency and stability of sticking to one career rather than risk moving around.
- 76 percent preferred the stability of living in one place long term.
- 72 percent of participants took part in zero-risk activities.
- 66 percent tended to stick to those they already knew to avoid taking social chances.

What Is Risk Aversion vs. Risk Management?

Risk aversion is the tendency to steer clear of uncertainty due to a low tolerance for potential loss or discomfort. In contrast, risk management involves acknowledging risk, analyzing it, evaluating the potential outcomes, and making informed decisions while actively monitoring the situation. It's not about avoiding risk; it's about navigating it with intention.

When I began hosting my podcast, I spoke with people from all walks of life. Some had put their personal lives on hold to dive into entrepreneurship. Others chose a more minimalist path, living simply to savor life's quieter joys. What I discovered through these conversations is that there's no universal "right" way to approach risk. Our life experiences, values, and circumstances all shape how we view and respond to it, whether we lean toward caution or embrace the unknown.

As with most things in life, how we choose to manage risk is a personal decision, but that choice can have a ripple effect, influencing many other areas, including those tied to our happiness. The way we handle uncertainty can shape our emotional well-being, relationships, career paths, and more.

That said, it raises a bigger question: what actually makes a country the happiest in the world? What factors contribute to collective joy and well-being on a national scale? Is risk management or risk aversion an integral part of the happiness formula for countries?

To find out, let's take a look at Finland, which has been ranked as the happiest country on Earth for six consecutive years.

Frank Martela, a philosopher and psychology researcher focused on the foundations of happiness, is a lecturer at Aalto University in Finland and the author of A Wonderful Life: Insights on Finding a Meaningful Existence. In a January 2023 article published by CNBC, Martela outlined three key things that people in Finland don't do, habits that may help explain why Finland consistently ranks as one of the happiest countries in the world.

- **We don't compare ourselves to our neighbors.** Focus more on what makes you happy and less on looking successful.

- **We don't overlook the benefits of nature.** Studies show that spending time in nature increases our vitality and well-being and gives us a sense of personal growth.

- **We don't break the community circle of trust.** Martela mentions that "Research shows that the higher the levels of trust within a country, the happier its citizens will be."

A 2022 study known as "The Lost Wallet" tested how people around the world respond when faced with a moral choice: return a lost wallet or keep it. Researchers dropped 192 wallets across sixteen global cities. In Helsinki, 11 out of 12 wallets were returned, an impressive show of honesty and social trust. In the United States, by contrast, only about half made it back to their owners. Interestingly, the U.S. has also seen a decline in its happiness ranking, falling from 15th in 2023 to 23rd. While many media outlets attribute this drop to rising economic inequality across generations, it's worth noting that the U.S. economy is growing faster than Finland's.

So, what's the difference? In a 2024 article in *The Atlantic*, Jedediah Britton-Purdy writes, "Trust isn't something that emerges naturally from a well-functioning society; people have to build it through hard work."

Does that mean you need to pack up and move to Finland? Not at all. What it does suggest is that happiness and well-being are closely tied to the social fabric we help create. Building trust, practicing kindness, and showing care in our everyday interactions, starting with our own neighborhoods, can make a meaningful impact. Small actions ripple outward and contribute to a stronger, more connected community.

Furthermore, in a 2013 *New York Times* opinion piece, Arthur Brooks stated, "Social scientists have caught the butterfly. After forty years of research, they attribute happiness to three major sources: genes, events, and values." In many of his talks, he emphasizes that genes make up a significant part of this equation. If that's true, then why even bother trying?

Even though genes play a significant role, there are other factors that influence our happiness. Constantly chasing happiness often has the opposite effect. Happiness isn't a fixed destination or a single emotion; it's more like a cloud drifting across the sky, appearing and fading naturally. In fact, it's a spectrum of feelings rather than just one. The key to cultivating happiness lies in creating a mental framework for it. You define the life you want to live, use that vision as your anchor, and work toward maintaining it.

By focusing on small, healthy habits, appreciating the little moments, and building trust and care within ourselves, we can extend this sense of well-being to our close relationships and then to our wider communities. Simple gestures, a smile, a hello, a wave, might seem small but can mean the world to someone feeling isolated. These acts not only brighten others' days but also bring us moments of peace and contentment. Instead of waiting for grand awakenings or big changes, happiness often shows up quietly, in the small moments we least expect.

As a society, we must teach this to our children. Some schools already incorporate mindfulness programs that encourage gratitude, presence, focus, and happiness. It's vital that we advocate for these changes to support future generations; the ripple effect will touch us all.

Learning about happiness isn't enough; wisdom comes from how we apply that knowledge. One powerful way to spread happiness is through kindness. Acts of kindness done without expecting anything in return can create a chain reaction, touching lives far beyond the initial gesture. Generosity and kindness have been scientifically shown to boost happiness, not only in others but within ourselves too.

Happiness fluctuates for all of us, and that's perfectly normal; it's part of being human. This is why I like to think of happiness as a frequency, as the number of waves that we can experience at any given point. It's not exact. It's not precise. It's a frequency; it's the present moment.

Beyond the research, studies, and science, what better way to capture the joy of the present moment than through the timeless words of William Henry Davies:

"Leisure"

What is this life if, full of care,
We have no time to stand and stare?— No time to stand
beneath the boughs, And stare as long as sheep and
cows: No time to see, when woods we pass, Where squir-
rels hide their nuts in grass: No time to see, in broad
daylight, Streams full of stars, like skies at night: No
time to turn at Beauty's glance,
And watch her feet, how they can dance: No time to wait
till her mouth can Enrich that smile her eyes began?
A poor life this if, full of care,
We have no time to stand and stare.

5

WHAT HAPPENED TO
THE RENEGADE?

Knowing yourself is the beginning of all wisdom.
—ARISTOTLE

A t this point in time, I now know just one thing to be certain: the renegade still lives within me, and I'm thankful for it. It's kept me alive; it's made me who I am today and it has empowered me to stand firmly for what I believe in, to stand firmly by my renegade beliefs. I recognize how much I've grown, yet many questions remain unanswered. No matter how long we live, we'll never have all the answers, and that's intentional. After all, how dull would life be if our sense of wonder and curiosity ever faded away?

A Roller Coaster of Life Changes

As I rode life's roller coaster, it suddenly threw me some unexpected twists and turns. In September 2022, I received the call no one ever wants to hear: "Marita, your father has had a heart attack." As I write this sentence, I'm sitting in the Fort Lauderdale airport, trying to board a plane back to New Jersey after visiting him. Since Hurricane Fiona swept through the southern part of the island, getting home from Puerto Rico has been nearly impossible. Now, as I finally leave Puerto Rico, the island remains devastated, still without power or water. I'm exhausted, sleep-deprived, and feel a panic attack building as the plane doors begin to close. The space seemed to close in on me, I struggled to take a deep breath, and when I glanced at my watch, my heart rate was racing. I texted Isabela, hoping she could help calm me down, but nothing seemed to work. Sitting by the window, I pushed past the people next to me, desperate to get out.

You can ask to get off the plane, but once the doors are closed, only a marshal can escort you out. Or so they told me, right before I realized 'asking nicely' doesn't beat federal air travel laws. Honestly, I can't remember the last time I felt so out of sorts.

I hadn't spoken to my father for an entire year before his heart attack. The last time we saw each other was back in October 2021, when he came to visit me and my family for his birthday. He'd been going through a rough time since losing his twin brother, and I wanted to lift his spirits. I offered to cover his flight so he could visit us, planned a nice dinner in NYC, and looked forward to enjoying the fall foliage together in the New Jersey mountains, where we had recently bought a home. After checking in with

Isabela, I gave him a call. He was genuinely excited and agreed to come for six days with his long-term girlfriend.

We prepped for the visit, planned outings, made the guest room cozy, and tried to anticipate their needs. But nothing prepared us for what actually unfolded. It became clear, almost immediately, how much he was struggling. The grief had weighed heavily on him, and his depression had deepened. His physical health had also declined, and his mental illness was taking a visible toll.

Out of genuine concern, I offered him my balance board to help with his unsteady walking, hoping it might ease some of the physical strain he was clearly under. But he quickly dismissed the gesture, insisting he didn't need any help.

I didn't push the issue again, but by the end of the trip, it was obvious he was ready to leave. We had a few tense moments— mostly around him wanting to use a wheelchair constantly or barely walking at all when we went out. I was frustrated. It felt like he was giving up on life, and in a moment of honesty, I voiced that frustration. I didn't press too hard, though, his long-term girlfriend, who'd come with him, seemed to reinforce his dependency. She had taken on the role of caretaker, and truthfully, it always seemed like she preferred it that way—as if him needing her gave their relationship purpose, but I think it made it easier for him to live with constant illness.

Eventually, I decided to stop pushing and just make the best of what time we had left on the trip. But when it came time for them to leave, my father didn't say goodbye. He didn't hug me. He just hobbled inside the airport to find a wheelchair, and I sat in the car, watching through the glass doors as they slid shut behind him. I drove off. We didn't speak again for nearly a year.

Neither of us picked up the phone. I had tried to do something meaningful for him, for us, but in the end, I was left feeling let down. To make things worse, I later found out he had told my brothers that Isabela and I had treated him poorly during the visit. That hit hard. What I had hoped would be a moment of healing only deepened the divide between us. I tried not to take it personally. I knew there were deeper issues at play; his depression was taking over more and more every day.

After getting the news that my father had a heart attack, after nearly a year of silence between us, I jumped out of bed, heart racing, unsure of what to do next. I scrambled to find a flight to Puerto Rico, and when Isabela and I finally secured one, she had to pack my bag while I rushed through a quick shower. As she dropped me off at the airport, the weight of it all finally hit me.

Would I even make it in time to say goodbye? My flight was delayed—then canceled. I was running through JFK in a panic, desperately searching for anyone from the airline who could help. Eventually, I found a woman at the counter, and as I explained the situation, her eyes welled up with tears. She told me it made her think of her own parents, as she had experienced a similar situation. Moved by the moment, she searched the system and somehow found one last-minute seat to Puerto Rico. I thanked her, then sprinted to the gate and boarded just in time.

I landed in Puerto Rico, where my mom, aunt, and older brother were waiting to pick me up. It was late, so there was nothing left to do but get some rest and prepare to head to the hospital first thing in the morning. When we arrived at the hospital, I made my way to the intensive care unit. The place felt cold and worn-down, with peeling paint on the walls from water damage. Despite some patients having been there for weeks, all they had separating them was a thin curtain.

With every step I took, my heart pounded faster and faster. I turned the corner and walked in. His eyes widened, and a smile broke across his face. I could see the relief wash over him. Then he began to sob and said, "I thought I'd never see you again, Marita."

I responded, "Don't cry, Dad. It's okay. I'm here now," struggling to hold back my own tears. I was grasping for strength in a moment when I felt none.

That evening, I sat on the porch of my mother's house, watching the clouds drift slowly across the sky. I closed my eyes and took a moment to meditate. Receiving news like that can change your life in an instant. Suddenly, the world feels vast and overwhelming, and you feel small and insignificant within it. No matter what I was going through, life around me carried on as usual: people getting dressed, grabbing their morning coffee, heading to work, and taking their kids to school. For them, it was just another ordinary day. For me, it was a day I would never forget. Losing someone, or even just the thought of losing someone, creates a void filled with unanswered questions and a haunting sense that there was never enough time. Because, truly, we never have enough time.

After nearly five days, my father began to improve. They moved him to a regular room, and he asked me to bring a few things before I arrived at the hospital. I went to the market to pick up the juices and snacks he wanted and brought them to him. He seemed like himself again. Since I was leaving the next day, we shared a hug, exchanged "I love you" and "I'll see you soon," and then I headed out.

The next morning, he was able to leave the hospital and head home.

On my way back to New Jersey, I couldn't find a direct flight. The storm that swept through the island had thrown the airlines into chaos, with countless canceled flights to catch up on. So, I had to take a connecting flight through Fort Lauderdale. I decided to spend a night with my cousins in Miami to rest before making the final leg home.

Then, just one day after landing in Fort Lauderdale, I got a call near midnight—my father had suffered a stroke, and the ambulance was rushing him to the hospital again. A few hours later, he had another heart attack. In the span of one week, he endured a massive heart attack, a stroke, and then a second heart attack. His body, which he never really treated kindly, held on just long enough to keep him alive. Since then, my father hasn't been able to speak.

In the days that followed, he underwent a tracheostomy, was placed on a ventilator, received a feeding tube, and carried several bruises on his arm from frequent blood transfusions. The image of him being kept alive by machines haunted me for days. When I finally returned to New Jersey, I sat with my wife at the kitchen island, sobbing. I was overwhelmed fearing I would never see or speak to him again, that even though his body remained alive, the father I knew was gone forever.

The thought made me feel like a lost child wandering alone in a store, unsure whether to turn left or right, desperate to find my parent, and convinced I was forever lost. It was like being caught in the middle of a storm with nothing to hold onto, completely powerless. I kept telling my wife that not speaking to him for a year sounded terrible in theory, but my last memory of him was buying him a plane ticket to visit us for his birthday. If I had kept receiving his calls during that year, the pain in my heart might have been even harder to bear.

Looking back, I wish I had a stronger relationship with him and more than just one day to try to rebuild it. I wanted us to move forward, but like when a child grows into an adult, family bonds change. Since we never really had a solid foundation to start with, building one in a hospital was even more difficult.

Within a month, I returned to Puerto Rico to see my father once more. By then, he had been in the ICU on life support for over five weeks.

As I walked down the hospital halls toward the elevator, my hands trembled and my heart pounded like a drum in my chest. A chill ran through my entire body. I wasn't sure how I'd react to seeing him bedridden, unable to speak, unable to be himself. When I reached the ICU and stepped into his room, he looked different. He had lost weight, hadn't shaved, his nails were overgrown, and his eyes seemed lost, as if he didn't recognize me.

I tried to speak, but didn't want him to see me upset. My voice trembled, and I feared the sadness in my eyes might frighten him. I asked him to squeeze my hand if he knew it was me, Marita. He did, holding my hand tightly, refusing to let go. I stayed with him for hours as he drifted in and out of sleep, the TV quietly humming in the background.

The hospital had introduced a music therapy program, and a woman would come play her violin for us. The gentle, soft strains of classical music made everything feel even more real. It stirred something deep inside me, and sometimes I had to step out. I would retreat to the lobby, quietly crying, hidden from the other visitors who were there for their own loved ones. I found a secluded corner with five chairs, shielded by columns so no one could see me.

I had never cried like that before, so raw and overwhelming that I'd forget to breathe between wiping away tears and cradling my face in my hands. I kept wishing none of this was happening. Questions swirled in my mind: Why are we here? How did it come to this? I knew the end was near, but denial washed over me in waves of anger and despair. I thought, if only the doctors could do more, if only they could heal him enough, maybe we'd have time to seek out more specialists across the island. Did the doctors even know what they were doing?

As I walked back to his room, I noticed that the rooms beside his held others in similar states. Through a glass window, I saw a young patient lying there with her eyes closed, looking so peaceful. I wondered how she had ended up there. It made me reflect on how we often take the simplest moments for granted, walking the dog, sharing a meal with a loved one, or browsing a bookstore filled with the stories of others.

I stayed on the island for five days, visiting him every day for nearly seven hours. We watched TV together, and I talked to him, asking questions. He would respond by squeezing my hand.

They kept him sedated to ease his pain, which meant some days he was barely awake enough to squeeze my hand. One day, he kept trying to focus on his vitals. He seemed anxious as his heart health was declining and the machine was constantly beeping. As a doctor, I thought he wanted to understand what was happening. I took a photo of the monitor, zoomed in on my phone, and showed it to him. I asked, "Is this what you want to see? I don't fully understand it, but I can call a nurse if you're worried."

He tried to open his eyes wide but then, in what felt like despair, slowly closed them again. Honestly, I was too afraid to ask why he looked so worried and hopeless. It was as if death was quietly knocking on his door while I was in denial, he seemed to understand what lay ahead. As the days went by, the continuous sedation took its toll, eventually causing cognitive decline. Gradually, he lost the ability to even squeeze my hand.

After five days, I visited him one last time before heading to the airport. I don't think I fully grasped the weight of that moment, but I remember not wanting to leave the room. I was overwhelmed by a mix of fear and anguish. I hugged him, told him I loved him, and promised I'd be back soon, though I didn't yet realize I wouldn't be able to keep that promise. As I walked away slowly, I kept looking back through the window to see him. I turned the corner, and the beige automatic doors slid open to reveal a cold, empty hallway leading to the parking elevator.

When I got home, I was trapped in a constant state of anxiety, dreading the call I knew would shatter my world. Every time the phone rang, my heart would race, skipping a beat until I finally answered. My older brother and I spoke with the doctors many times, hoping for any possible treatments. As the months went by and without a living will, they asked if we would consider disconnecting the machines keeping him alive to see how his body would respond. I felt more angry than sad—how could I make that decision? How could I choose whether he lives or dies? Why would you ask me this? The doctors were running out of options, and to them, this was simply one more possibility to consider.

One cold winter Sunday, January 22nd at noon, I was driving up my street to have lunch with a neighbor when my phone rang. It was my older brother, Mario Jr. I fumbled trying to pull it out of my pocket as he called again. Finally, I answered.

"Marita, the doctor called. Dad just passed away."

Silence. I didn't say a word.

"Marita, are you there?"

My brother's voice was shaky, barely able to get the words out. It was the call I had been dreading.

On the other end, Isabela was calling, as I continued to speak with my brother. Mario Jr. quickly said, "We need to tell Sam."

I just couldn't do it, and I told him so. In the midst of his own pain, my brother Sam had chosen to blame others for our father's decline. I'm not judging him, but I knew I couldn't be on the receiving end of that. I couldn't be there for him the way I wanted to. I realized I couldn't hold together the world we once knew—for both of us.

After a long conversation, Mario Jr. said he was booking a flight to Puerto Rico that very day. I didn't understand the urgency, but he wanted to get the funeral arrangements started right away. For the past four months, Mario Jr. had taken the lead, keeping close with the doctors, managing bills, and basically running our father's affairs while he was incapacitated. He didn't have to do it all himself, I offered to help but he continued.

I understood that, for his own peace, he needed to close this chapter. The pain and anxiety had become unbearable for him, while I was still barely processing what had just happened, I couldn't fully grasp that my father was gone, that I would never again hear his voice when I picked up the phone. One thought kept echoing in my mind: I would never be able to say the word "Dad" again. It all felt so final. I was completely grief-stricken. The emotional numbness hit harder than I expected. Everything around me seemed to move in slow motion. After talking to Mario Jr., Isabela called again and told me my sister-in-law had reached out. I told her Dad had passed away. She cried, said "I love you," and told me to come home when I was ready. Somehow, despite it all, I still went out to lunch with my neighbor. I couldn't and wouldn't accept the news. I wasn't ready to face the truth. I knew that the moment I walked back into the house, reality would crash down on me.

After lunch, I walked into the house and told Isabela I was going to take a shower. As the water poured over my head, I clutched my face and cried, deep, uncontrollable sobs. The next few days passed in a haze. All I remember is waking up each morning for about a week, thinking, Whose life is this? It didn't feel like mine. Losing my father felt like being trapped in a dream I was waiting to wake up from. They say grief comes in waves, and it's true. I often find myself thinking about him and what might have been. I've had many dreams where we speak and it feels so real.

As I prepared to travel to Puerto Rico, I felt like a lost child all over again. I struggled with the simplest tasks, navigating TSA, paying for a meal, helpless and overwhelmed. I moved through the airport in a daze, slow and lumbering, until I finally made it to the gate.

As we began our descent and the plane's wheels lowered, I glanced out the window and saw the waves gently rolling onto the shore of Isla Verde. The ocean's steady, calming rhythm had always been a source of comfort for me. When the wheels touched down, the familiar clapping and cheering began—we had arrived in Puerto Rico.

But this time, it felt different. The island felt empty, desolate. I had once flown here to say goodbye to my grandfather; now, I was here to do the same with my father. The island that was once my home and full of family was now getting smaller every year. Ironically, that is the reason why I moved out of the island in the first place; it felt too small as I was growing up, and now with family members passing away it was actually getting smaller.

No matter where life takes me, how I feel about the island, or how many times I move, Puerto Rico will always be my first home. Over the years, my love for Puerto Rico has only grown stronger. Like the song by Fiel De La Vega says, *Boricua en la luna*—"Puerto Rican even on the moon."

Dad passed away on a Sunday, and we had the wake Thursday all day because Sam and my dad's long-time girlfriend insisted that it's how he would have wanted it. I'm not sure if that was true, but I didn't have the strength to question it. The planning, the wake, and everything in between were filled with many disagreements and grief as we all battled with the heartbreak in our own ways.

Dad didn't leave a will with his last wishes, so we buried him in the National Cemetery with the hopes that it was what he would have wanted. The ceremony seemed endless, and as I stood to read the eulogy that I'd spent hours perfecting, I could barely keep it together. My sentences were drawn out and peppered with pauses, all while I was attempting not to shake. When I finished, I kissed the casket and walked back to my seat.

As the men and women in uniform fired their rifles into the sky, each shot echoed like a drumbeat against my grief, intensifying it with every round. The mournful notes of "Taps" from a lone bugler added a solemn beauty to the ceremony. Still, as they carried the casket away, I found myself repeating to myself again and again, "It wasn't his time... not yet," clinging to a sense of control I never had. The truth was, it wasn't him who wasn't ready to go; it was me who wasn't ready to let him go.

The day arrived for us to leave Puerto Rico, and as Isabela and I waited to board, I pulled out my phone to send one final message. I texted my dad's number, "I'm leaving, Dad. Love you." He used to ask me to message him before takeoff, and even though he wouldn't read it this time, I felt like I owed him that one last goodbye.

As the weeks passed, I found myself longing for just one more conversation with him. If I'd had the chance, I would've said, "I'm so sorry you died alone in that hospital room. That was never what I wanted for you. I'm sorry I wasn't there when it happened. I should've been. Because despite everything, I've managed to forgive you, Dad."

I know he spent much of his life searching for happiness, starting over again and again with marriages, careers, new beginnings. And there I was, always in the middle, silently hoping for the kind of relationship between us that never came to be. My brothers grieved in their own ways, but I often felt alone in my mourning, like no one could truly understand what I was feeling.

At different points in their lives, they had lived under the same roof as Dad. I never had that. I didn't know what it was like to wait for him to come home from work or to sit down for family dinners in the evenings. There was a version of him they got to know, a part of his life I was never part of.

I was thirty-six when he died, but inside, I felt like a six-year-old, raw, abandoned, angry. Grief hits in irrational waves: anger, envy, longing. I couldn't help but look at others who still had their parents and felt this jealousy that made no logical sense, but was all too real.

To navigate the pain, I turned to memoirs written by those who'd also lost their parents suddenly, desperate to find a mirror of my own sadness. I hoped that in their words, I might feel a little less alone. Because grief, I've come to learn, often feels like walking endlessly through a narrow hallway, lungs tight, heart heavy, burdened by the absence of someone who can never return.

I was living in a constant state of anxiety, consumed by worry for mami and titi, silently begging the universe, *'Please, just give me more time with them.'* At the same time, every time Isabela left for work, I tracked her location on my phone, my mind racing through worst-case scenarios. The thought of losing anyone else I loved was simply unbearable. As the months passed, I realized life never returned to what it once was. I was still me, but something had shifted—emotionally and mentally, I was evolving, slowly learning how to live again.

For months, I found myself drawn to Salsa music, searching for ways to feel closer to my dad through the foods we used to enjoy together and visits to the places he loved. But as time passed, a quiet realization settled in: I didn't really know him. I didn't know his favorite color, his biggest pet peeve, the regrets he may have carried, what led him to become a doctor, why he wanted a family, or how he truly saw the world. That realization brought a different kind of grief, not just for the loss of his presence, but for the conversations we never had, the questions left unasked.

Nonetheless, today as I look in the mirror, I keep noticing a little bit of him in me. What were once the things that I most hated about myself are the things that bring me closer to him now that he's gone. How ironic life can be?

His absence throughout my childhood took years to unpack, but I've come to realize that it shaped my resilience and sharpened my ability to adapt. Without meaning to, he taught me one of the most important lessons of my life: how to be resourceful. Out of that early adversity, a seed was planted, and over time, it grew into something meaningful. I now see it as a powerful and beautiful lesson.

As for my mother and aunt, they still live in my grandfather's home in Puerto Rico, a house that shaped me, sheltered me from childhood through young adulthood, and taught me countless life lessons. Now retired, they are the only family I have left on the island since my father's passing.

As life would have it, my relationship with my mother began to shift after their 70th birthday celebration in 2018, years before my father passed away. I had organized the party, but shortly after, a disagreement between us surfaced, casting a shadow over what was meant to be a celebration. My mother has never been one to handle confrontation well, but her friend who attended the party was outspoken about gay people, making comments that were in very poor taste. On top of that, what probably hurt the most was that Mom had shared pictures of other weddings she had recently attended but somehow neglected to share mine. This made me think that, deep down, she still had not fully made peace with the person I am and that, in some way, she agreed with her friend's comments. This only escalated things further as we continued discussing what happened that evening. A few days later, her cousin Glenda inserted herself into the situation by sending me what could only be described as a manifesto. It wasn't a warm note or an attempt to bridge understanding even though this had nothing to do with her—it was a numbered list, lengthy and unfiltered, laying out all the ways in which I was, according to her, the worst daughter imaginable.

What hurt the most wasn't just the list itself; it was knowing that it contained personal details only my mother could have shared. It felt like my childhood mistakes and past missteps had been laid bare, put on display, as if no one could let go of who I used to be, the child who was hurting, trying to make sense of it all.

All written in Times New Roman, size 12, or maybe size 14. I mean, at least it wasn't Comic Sans. Comic Sans is the font equivalent of wearing socks with sandals. Gen Z might've made it trendy recently, but come on, is it really that cool?

Over the years, I've worked hard to process the pain and disappointment that email left behind. At first, it felt like a sharp sting to my heart, an unexpected blow that shook my confidence and made me question my worth. But with time, reflection, and a lot of self-compassion, I began to untangle the hurt from my sense of self. I learned to see that the pain wasn't a reflection of my value but rather a mirror of other people's limitations, a projection of their own limited perspectives. Now, with my mom and aunt as my only living ties to Puerto Rico and to my Puerto Rican and Cuban heritage, I find myself searching for a new path forward in my relationship with them, one rooted in presence and gratitude.

As long as they're here, I've made a commitment to visit them every six months. It's my way of nurturing the relationship we have now, focusing less on the past and more on creating meaningful moments in the present. During my visits, we play board games, take walks through the neighborhood, and wind down in the evenings with movies or a glass of wine shared among friends.

When it comes to my brothers, loss has quietly sent each of us down separate paths. We live far apart, and our age differences have placed us in different stages of life. As I continue forward, I've come to accept that we each need space, to grieve, to grow, and to figure out who we are without our father. Whether our paths will cross again in a meaningful way remains to be seen. Only time will tell, but the door remains open on my side if they choose to walk through it.

I've come to understand that even when you build the life you've always wanted, it doesn't shield you from sadness, fear, loss, or failure. These experiences are part of the journey, and without them, we wouldn't fully appreciate the beauty and depth of life's most meaningful moments.

We need to find meaning within ourselves and through our relationships, experiences, hopes, dreams, and fears. Yet in today's digital world, emotions can become fleeting trends, much like hobbies. Platforms like Instagram flood us with reels showcasing how we "should" feel in certain situations. While this creates a sense of shared experience, it can also make emotions feel generic, limiting our ability to connect with our own unique feelings or uncover personal meaning. Social media creators tap into relatable scenarios, but this often blinds us, leaving us all thinking, feeling, and saying the same things instead of embracing our individuality.

Listen to your renegade; it's the truest path to your authentic self.

I've grown and changed through the seasons of my life. In my mid-twenties, I dreamed of living in a bustling city filled with software engineers and startups. I spent my free time scouring Eventbrite for meetups where I could connect with others in the industry. I'd show up, swap business cards and LinkedIn profiles, and of course, enjoy the free pizza.

Entering my thirties, I discovered contemplative practices like mindfulness meditation and felt drawn to nature and the solitude it offers. I wanted to find clarity about what I truly needed and wanted in life. After selling our townhouse, we bought a home surrounded by mountains and woods, where birds greet the morning with song. Now, I can spend days at home, soaking in the peaceful quiet. The solitude no longer intimidates or frightens me—now, I crave it.

My tech career has blossomed far beyond what I once dreamed possible. Leading and mentoring others has become more than just a role, it's a calling. Balancing the pressures of the business while nurturing people's growth has been a challenging journey, but one filled with profound meaning. With each passing year,

I lead bigger and more diverse teams around the world. Once I stumble upon someone like me, someone with learning disabilities, struggling to find their way, I see an opportunity to embrace them with the kindness and understanding I longed for when I was in their shoes. It's a chance to create the support and compassion I wish had been there for me, and that brings deeper purpose to the work I do every day. For nearly thirteen years, I've walked the fast-moving corridors of tech, splitting my time between the restless energy of New York City and the innovation-charged air of Silicon Valley. I've worked across Series A, B, and C startups, each one a pressure cooker of ambition and uncertainty. I've weathered the intensity of rapid scaling, the quiet tension of pre-IPO nights, the whirlwind of acquisitions, and the rare clarity that comes with seeing a company go public. It's a path that's demanded resilience, a clear head, and an unwavering sense of purpose.

But perhaps the most meaningful part of that journey has been guiding others, mentoring those ready to lead, and coaching those still finding their footing. In helping them rise, I discovered a deeper, more enduring version of success.

And last but definitely not least, if you're seeking marriage advice, look no further than... well, another book. Jokes aside, after nearly eleven years with Isabela and seven years of marriage, I've come to realize I really don't have all the answers and I never will.

Marriage is a shared journey through life. Your successes become theirs, and theirs become yours. Your pain intertwines too, but the truth is, you can't always be the fixer or the rescuer, even if you want to be. What you can be is their rock, their listener, their sounding board, their support.

Think of marriage like a home: it requires regular care and upkeep. Without that attention, its value diminishes. A marriage demands the same kind of consistent effort to thrive. Carve out time to nurture it, and you'll witness the beautiful results it can bring.

My wife and I have found this by dedicating time each week for a gratitude session during our Sunday meal. We also create a shared vision to prepare for the year ahead. Our marriage isn't perfect. Some days, weeks, and months are wonderful, while others require hard work. As ever-evolving people, we've learned to fall in love with each other, year after year.

We've had to learn how to negotiate, compromise, let go of anger, and look past petty arguments to find the lessons they hold.

At my core, I will always be the same renegade—full of ideas, some of which make my wife raise an eyebrow or even roll her eyes. I've learned to embrace every version of myself: the past, the present, and the ones yet to come. Only time will tell what future me thinks of this book, but I hope she gives it a thumbs up, and maybe even a glowing review on Amazon or wherever. And if she doesn't, well, I hope you will.

Scars and Life Lessons

The scars we can't see are often the ones that take the longest to heal. Sometimes, those invisible wounds transform into powerful reminders, some so meaningful they became tattoos on my skin.

Shortly after meeting Isabela, I got a tattoo on my left bicep that reads, "Live Free." It's a personal reminder to live and love without limits.

On my left wrist, I have a power button tattoo. When people ask about it, I often say it's because I work in tech. But its true meaning goes much deeper; it's connected to my ADHD. Growing up, I was repeatedly told to sit still, be quiet, "you're too much," "be better," and to behave. As a child with ADHD, my compulsive behaviors would often take control, and even when I was told "no," I struggled to understand or stop them.

Those words echoed through school halls, my home, and my mind, leaving me feeling embarrassed and ashamed of who I was. Over time, I realized my ADHD is actually my superpower. When I need to hyperfocus or meet tight deadlines, I can accomplish in five hours what might take others an entire day.

On my right arm, I have a dog paw print, honoring all the four-legged family members who grounded me when life felt overwhelming. When everything seemed suffocating, they were the ones who helped me find my footing again.

And lastly, I have a simple stick figure meditating, a symbol of my daily medicine when life becomes overstimulating or when I feel the need to control everything around me.

I'm still the renegade at heart, but I've grown more at peace with life's cravings and temptations. Meditation taught me to see life through a different lens. It became a steady light in moments of darkness and doubt. In the end, it's you and your actions that shape the masterpiece you leave behind.

If you've made it to the end of this book, I want to close with something meaningful. Never forget where you come from, for gratitude has the power to nurture our mental, physical, and emotional well-being. Always remember to pay it forward; acts of kindness and service connect us deeply to others. And above all, never stop doing good in the world, because in giving, we find meaning, purpose, and the true essence of life.

Lately, I've been having a recurring, vivid dream. I find myself in the woods, unsure of exactly where I am, yet not feeling lost. A calm settles within me as a black bear approaches. I don't feel fear or intimidation; I neither run nor fight. It's as if I know this bear, and we peacefully coexist in the forest. The dream happened so often that I felt compelled to research what a black bear symbolizes in dreams. As I kept reading, the three main things that came forward were that black bears symbolize power, authority, change and the ability to move forward despite obstacles.

Today as I look into the mirror, I can see the scars from life lessons left behind. The sadness that once shadowed my eyes, born from years of hiding my true self, has finally lifted. What stares back now is the renegade inside me: alive and unwavering. I've come to understand that in this one life, happiness, fulfillment, purpose, and hope never needed to be checked off a list. The answers were always within me, carried quietly from the start.

Unmistakably and unapologetically, I will always be a renegade at heart, a renegade walking the endless path toward stillness, even if I sometimes take a detour for coffee... or to chase a squirrel.

Circa 2025

RESOURCES PER CHAPTER

- **Chapter 1**: The Values Worksheet
- **Chapter 2**: The Box Approach Template
- **Chapter 2**: The Mindful Renegade Journal Prompts
- **Chapter 2**: The Curated Spotify Playlist
- **Chapter 3**: Free Meditation Recording From Insight Timer

Learn more by visiting https://maritaespada.com
or scan the QR Code below:

ACKNOWLEDGMENTS

To my mother, who had love in her heart and the best intentions when raising me.

To my aunt and grandparents, who helped raise me in their own unique ways.

To my father, who taught me about resilience and that we cannot change people, only accept them for who and where they are.

To all my extended family, for being pages and chapters in my life that I will always remember.

To all my friends, you shaped chapters in my life, and I will be forever grateful.

To my official portrait photographers, though they didn't know it, Koko Guzman and my wonderful wife, Irene.

To my editor Jesse Winter and my book designer Sarah Lahay, thank you for your patience and guidance.

To the readers, thank you from the bottom of my heart for purchasing my book. I hope you enjoy reading it as much as I enjoyed writing it.

SOURCES

- Gabor Mate Interview with Tim Ferriss - Tim Ferriss Show (You Tube)

- How neuroplasticity helps us shape who we become | André Vermeulen | TEDxJohannesburg

- National Institutes of Health (NIH) - Brain Basics: Understanding Sleep

- Why Does the Brain Need So Much Power? New study shows why the brain drains so much of the body's energy. By Nikhil Swaminathan

- Finding Stillness At 95 MPH : Shawn Green at TEDxOrangeCoast (YouTube)

- Wisdom 2.0 Mindfulness Summit Interview: Phil Jackson, George Mumford & Jon Kabat-Zinn

- North Western Mutual Study- Planning & Progress Study 2019

- I'm a psychology expert in Finland, the No. 1 happiest country in the world—here are 3 things we never do. Frank Martela

www.ingramcontent.com/pod-product-compliance
Lightning Source LLC
Chambersburg PA
CBHW031512120626
46545CB00005B/1840